Belief Change
- The Book-

KISS
The Keep It Simple Series

Belief Change
~The Book~

**How-to Find and Transform
Hidden Beliefs
That Sabotage Success
and Defeat Your Dreams**

Janet Gentleman & Diana Torrence

for change everlasting…

Table of Contents

Disclaimer..ix

Introduction 1

Chapter 1   Energy of Belief...7

Chapter 2   Belief Change Exercise 17

Chapter 3   "THE DARK SIDE"...24

Chapter 4   SHARING YOUR INSIGHTS AND BENEFITS...........27

Chapter 5   Belief Change Exercise (BCE) Step 1.....................30

Chapter 6   Belief Change Exercise (BCE) Step 2.....................34

Chapter 7   Belief Change Exercise (BCE) Step 3.....................37

Chapter 8   Belief Change Exercise (BCE) Step 4.....................42

Chapter 9   Belief Change Exercise (BCE) Step 5.....................47

Chapter 10   Belief Change Exercise (BCE) Step 6.....................50

Chapter 11   Belief Change Exercise (BCE) Step 7....................58

Chapter 12   Belief Change Exercise (BCE) Step 8.....................62

Chapter 13   Belief Change Exercise (BCE) Step 9.....................65

Chapter 14   Belief Change Exercise (BCE) Step 10....................68

Chapter 15   What's next?..94

Disclaimer

This book is a general education service for anyone interested in the Belief Change Exercise (BCE).

As an express condition to using this book, you understand and agree to the following terms:

1. Book content is not a substitute for direct, personal, professional medical or psychological care and diagnosis. None of the exercises or activities mentioned in this book should be performed without clearance from your physician or mental health care provider.

2. There may be risks associated with participating in activities mentioned in this book for people in poor mental or emotional health or with pre-existing physical or mental health conditions.

3. Because these risks exist, you will not participate in such activities if you are in poor health or have a pre-existing mental, emotional or physical condition. If you choose to participate in these risks, you do so of your own free will and accord, knowingly and voluntarily assuming all risks associated with such activities.

4. You agree to hold this book, its owners, agents, and employees harmless from any and all liability for all claims for damages due to injuries, including attorney fees and costs, incurred by you or caused to third parties by you, arising out of the activities discussed in this book, excepting only claims for gross negligence or intentional tort.

5. You agree that any and all claims for gross negligence or intentional tort shall be settled solely by confidential binding arbitration per the American Arbitration Association commercial arbitration rules. All arbitration must occur in Collin County, Texas, USA, and Texas law shall govern. Arbitration fees and costs shall be split equally, and you are solely responsible for your own lawyer fees.

IF YOU DO NOT AGREE WITH THESE EXPRESS CONDITIONS, DO NOT USE THIS BOOK. YOUR USE OF THIS BOOK AND ANY PARTICIPATION IN ACTIVITIES MENTIONED IN THIS BOOK, MEAN THAT YOU ARE AGREEING TO BE LEGALLY BOUND BY THESE TERMS.

Introduction

How does your life, the life you experience right now, compare to the life you hoped and dreamed of living?

Have you sometimes felt trapped, hopeless, limited by life's circumstances and conditions?

Have you ever felt doomed to repeat the same relationships over and over again?

Or is life actually going well but you feel you would love to do better, go faster, and get more done with less effort…

What would you do, be, or have if only you could?

What would it be worth to you to discover a truly magical exercise that produced lasting and desirable changes in your current situation? Would it be worth a few hours of meditative thought and documentation?

If you answered yes and you are willing to invest the time, this book is for you!

Many of you read the book *The Secret* or watched the DVD[1]. It is all about The Law of Attraction and living life being, doing, and having anything you ask your "personal genie" to provide.

Many of you accepted its challenge to ask the Universe for $30,000.00 in 30 days from unexpected sources.

Or perhaps you made up your own personal 'Treasure Board' – a pictorial representation of your hopes, dreams, and desires. Some of you had amazing results while others were disappointed and disillusioned. Many experienced mixed results.

This book exists to help you understand and, if you choose, to redesign, the belief system that prevented you from being, doing or having your heart's desire.

The benefit to you, from completing the Belief Change Exercise (BCE) contained within includes:

1. Collapses *unconscious* energetic charges that haunt, limit, or are a barrier to a peaceful, fulfilling, and meaningful life experience – it *gets rid of the demons!*
2. Enables you to fulfill your destiny - accomplish that for which you aspire, hope, and desire!
3. Frees you to move to a higher level emotionally and spiritually – creates *silence* for the *presence* experience described in Eckhart Tolle's books[2].

My Story

I grew up in a dysfunctional but loving family – as did so many others – a hazard of the hectic lifestyles of the day and age. As a result I spent countless hours on various psychiatrist, psychologist and counselor's sofas resisting, hating and lamenting *something* only to leave their office believing I was worse off than when I entered. I then spent a small fortune exploring every alternative from gypsy spiritual counselors to intuitive medical professionals and from NLP to Holographic Repatterning to earning a Bachelor's Degree in Psychology and a Ministerial License as well as a multitude of other methodologies in between… Finally, I realized that each attempt to heal was one piece in my life's puzzle. What I learned was that no single practice held the *final* all-encompassing *solution* for all my problems. That makes sense! I did not accumulate all my limiting beliefs in one hour nor even in a weekend and I wasn't going to reframe or transform them *all* instantly … as I had hoped. I certainly fell prey to the microwave culture's mindset!

Norman Vincent Peale, the king of positive thinking, once said, "The only people who *do not* have problems reside in cemeteries." Profound, true, and strangely comforting! *Everybody* has problems, difficulties, and obstacles? *Obviously* the President of the US does but what about the Hiltons, the British royalty, movies stars? Surely their lives are nothing but fun and games with a little work mixed in here and there, but mostly fun and games! Right? If that were true the tabloids and paparazzi would be out of business!

Surely preachers and class presidents are immune or the family next door. Have you read the news lately?

I now peacefully accept that I will spend my adult life clearing accumulated debris. Debris being the *decisions or judgments* I made through immature, unaware or under-educated filters and all their resulting drama. And, I joyfully celebrate that the quality of my problems is much better than some of those I read about or hear about on the radio or television!

Peacefully accepting does not mean do nothing more to improve my state of mind and life conditions! What it does mean is that I now replace frantic endeavors to instantly heal my wounds with patient and interesting, sometimes surprising, exploration of layer removing exercises that I can do as a need arises. What I gained from this shift is amazing insight into my psyche. Working through the exercise I learn what drives many of my behaviors negative *and* positive. Most importantly, like cleaning out the closet, I can keep what fits me and recycle what no longer serves my needs!

This book is a collaborative effort with a woman, now a dear friend, who provided me with this exercise that I can work on my own, in secret or to share – an exercise that effectively peels the layers and exposes those insane driving beliefs that torment and torture as well as the powerful, enabling beliefs that I can and do leverage toward achievements and personal fulfillment.

As a result of her 38 years in personal development work, about 12 years ago my co-author Diana Torrence developed a highly effective and successful workshop; Transcend Your Limitations. This program teaches people how to handle beliefs in paired together counseling partnerships, and it gets extraordinary results when applied well. But the amount of training and practice involved slowed up the process of making it available to large numbers of people to unearth their beliefs and banish them from their universe.

Consequently, Diana considered how to fine-tune the procedure even more, so that someone with a strong intention and focus could tackle it on their own. After simplifying and testing procedures already in use by Belief Change Facilitation facilitators with their clients, the Belief Change Exercise (hereafter known as BCE), which includes the unique specially created Step 10, was born. As one of the first people to try it out, I can assure you from personal experience, it works!

The book is laid out exactly as it would be presented in either a workshop or a one-on-one counseling session. It is intended for you to study a segment and then do the step, which often includes writing out the answers to various questions, through a total of ten steps until you reach a completion point.

Providing you follow our guidelines and apply each exercise thoroughly you can expect to receive astonishing results. That being said, as with all else in life, *"garbage in, garbage out"* applies! What you receive from working through this exercise is proportional to your effort completing it. This is GOOD news! You are completely in the driver's seat.

It is also important to note that this exercise is likely to be an emotional journey. This is normal! Be prepared to be comfortable in whatever pain and trauma that surfaces, and look for the good that came from them to add to the amazing being you are today. A box of Kleenex along with colored felt pens, highlighters, pen or pencil, and paper are staples of the Belief Change Exercise. A journal to record date, time, and insights is optional but highly recommended.

The Flip Chart images included in this book are from the interactive program that facilitates participants through each step of the BCE. We have included them to aid your learning process. In the workshop environment in which we use SuperLearning[3] techniques, they are a vital part of absorbing and retaining the key information and achieving competence. For maximum benefit, we encourage you, our reader, to copy the charts from the book onto sheets of paper using multiple, bright colors – it can help you to better understand the concepts and procedure.

To genuinely receive the full benefit of the Belief Change Exercise presented in this book, honor your body's needs. To be able to reveal insights it is essential that your body be fully hydrated, nourished and if possible free of chemistry-altering substances such as alcohol, or drugs either prescribed or otherwise obtained. It is wise to do the exercise in an environment free of potential interruption and excessive background noise. Your body wants to work in sync with your mind to provide you the most profound, enlightening experience that you need for where you are in your life journey. Your mind and body need your support to succeed.

The most important piece of advice I can share personally is to commit to yourself to work all the way through all ten steps; then honor your commitment. Happy journey! jan

Chapter 1

Energy of Belief

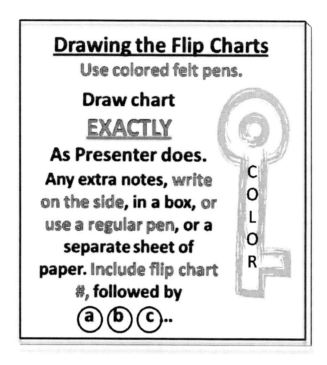

To optimize learning –
copy flip charts with multi-colored pens not Black & White.

The theory and background of beliefs and their impact on your life is extremely complex and remains open to study and opinion. What we offer are simplified definitions, illustrations and exercises that *we* can understand and we hope make sense to you as well.

Belief: an idea, the product of a judgment or decision individually or collectively held to be absolute, true and real. Can be argued and validated by evidence that appears real and indisputable.

What are Beliefs?

What are beliefs? They are the decisions and judgments that make up perceptions we hold as *truths*. They come from your parents, your culture, and a few are globally inspired, but most are from you! The majority of these beliefs are the product of your personal judgments and decisions made as a result of experiences and events you either were personally involved in or you observed. Again, this is *good* news! Because you made them or adopted them (i.e., became attached to a particular belief that presented as a good solution to a seemingly irresolvable situation) you can change them!

Why do we have a belief system?

If a belief system is all made-up stuff, why do you have a belief system? It is essential because we all live in a world filled with sensory information. A multitude of sights, sounds, feelings, tastes and scents bombard us in any given moment. In the process of designing life on planet earth as we know it, Infinite Intelligence recognized we had to have a way to filter what would otherwise be overwhelming and unnecessary.

A *belief* appears to *serve* you in some way important to you – typically appearing to protect you in some way from *pain* and *discomfort*.

Often it is a decision made in the midst of an emotionally charged experience or a judgment made about the situation that allows you to maintain your self-esteem and/or make sense of it.

A belief is one way of handling what appears un-resolvable.

How a BELIEF appears to BETTER your LIFE

Disordered, STUCK, area -- Very hard to face up to or deal with, **lots of problems.**

Adopts belief, *"If I ignore it, it will go away"*, *"If I try to be financially free, I'll be too busy to enjoy it."*

How does a belief system work?

There is an amazing mind-opening exercise that Tony Robbins uses to illustrate the power of filters. Look around the room you are in and make a mental note of everything you see that is green. Then, close your eyes and tell me everything you saw that was blue.

If you are like most people your brain screams *"What?! You told me to focus on green so I focused on green."* Most people notice little else but what they are looking for. Consequently, in this exercise, most people cannot list many blue items in their surroundings and are amazed when they look around and see all they missed that was there.

Similarly, you can look around and see all that is *bad* in your life or you can focus on what is *good*. Like in the Tony Robbins *Green/Blue Exercise*[4], whichever you focus on you will notice the most. Although both "good" and "bad" exist simultaneously always, over time we train our belief system to filter out the one on which we are not focused!

Another way to understand this concept is to consider how many cell phone calls bounce off a cellular tower at any given moment. Hundreds, thousands and yet, you don't hear any of them except the one directed to your particular handset?

All those sound waves are there in the atmosphere; why can't you hear them? The simplified answer is because, to hear them requires a sophisticated instrument – your handset - designed to pick up only the exact frequency calls directed to your cell phone identification number and to ignore all others. Radios and televisions also filter out all but a selected frequency.

Your belief system works like the tuner knob: it focuses only on whatever it determines to be relevant to your life experience. Its purpose, to evaluate and differentiate what is meaningful and useful from that which is either neutral or a threat.

Once your ego[5] – acting as gatekeeper - determines the event is either "good" or "bad" for you, it then activates the physical features that provide us with essential ingredients for whatever you decide is an appropriate response – action. Action includes a combination of thought or self-talk, spoken words and behavior.

Most of us have heard stories of a mother who lifted a heavy car off her trapped child. Her ability to suddenly demonstrate super-human strength was a direct result of her belief that her child's life was in danger. It is also evidence of the body's amazing resourcefulness to provide on demand. The intensity of the emotion attached to the mother's belief triggered an adrenaline hormone surge to her muscles and enabled her to lift beyond her normal ability.[6]

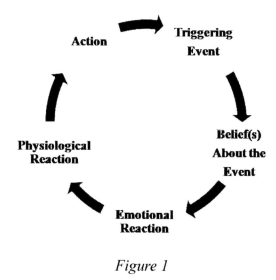

Figure 1

Figure 1. Simplified illustration of how beliefs work. It starts with an **event** which activates a **belief** which triggers an **emotional response** that causes a **physiological response** initiating an **action**.

In a healthy person, beliefs *always* trigger an emotional then physiological response that *always* initiates a decision on action. Sometimes responses go unnoticed, but they happen. Similarly, action can be either visible or audible and obvious or hidden within your mind and body yet is inherent in the nature of the belief system and purpose.

The hidden actions typically can manifest as illness, aches or injury. Louise Hay's book *Heal Your Life*[7] effectively illustrates the link between unresolved beliefs and your physical body. More importantly, she shares strategies for replacing their destructive influence with constructive and empowering beliefs. This works well for beliefs that are more obvious and easy to identify. The Belief Change Exercise, hereafter known as BCE, in this book works to expose hidden and deep-seated limiting beliefs providing you the opportunity for their resolution.

At this point it is important to note that not all beliefs are limiting or harmful. In fact, it is your empowering and beneficial beliefs that cause your success. The really good news about beliefs is that you can change them, transform them into empowering and beneficial beliefs as your knowledge and understanding grows and expands. Please note: **You *can choose* beliefs that *serve* you** – in other words: beliefs that help you reach goals or get what you want. Once you understand how a belief is created you will see how easy it is to redesign a belief system that launches and energizes you to fulfill your heart's desires.

How a belief system is created

So how is a belief system created? It is *built* either through repetition or adoption.

Repetition: You have the basic concept of how beliefs work: event leads to belief which triggers an emotional response activating a supportive physiological response resulting in an action. And then it begins again.

The *system* is built every time the event repeats (or one perceived as *similar* occurs) and is confirmed either good or bad according to your standard. For this role, Ego as gatekeeper, serves very much like an administrative assistant and orders the vast wealth of information your mind receives into a mental file cabinet for easy and timely access. It stacks newly acquired, additional supporting evidence in the file of similar previous experiences. This process happens so fast you do not even notice it[8].

How many times in your life have you heard statements like the following:

- Money is the root of all evil.
- Money doesn't grow on trees.
- The good die young.
- Cancer runs in my family.
- Children should be seen and not heard.
- You can't do *that* because_____...

What do these have in common? They are all examples of beliefs typical people adopt from their culture, from their family, from their religion, from their community and so on. These are only a few examples of many that are the little voice, like the one in the back of your head, that won't let you do what you really want or are meant to do! When it stops us from doing something *bad* we call it conscience; it has other names when it prevents *good* action: "self-talk", "the voice", "mom-on-your-shoulder", etc.

Our exercise helps you identify beliefs and their *effect* on your life. How do beliefs play out in your life? How do you *experience* them?

The first way is *results*. When you want to accomplish something specific and something entirely or moderately different shows up, it may be a clue that a limiting, or *fixed* belief activated. For example:

- Failed attempt for promotion
- Relationship failure
- Weight loss failure
- Financial failure

Fixed Belief: an idea, the product of a judgment or decision individually or collectively held to be absolute, true and real. Can be argued and validated by evidence that appears real and indisputable.

It feels unsafe and unwise to believe otherwise. The danger and logic of it seems obvious and clear.

TO A TRULY FIXED BELIEF
You feel it would be
- **unwise to get rid of it**
  OR even that you might cease to exist
- **You might even feel it is**
  part of you, or who you are

The second really powerful clue to the presence of a limiting or *fixed* belief is a pattern. When you try to accomplish something over and over again and keep getting something different that is a powerful clue. I.e.,

- Consistently overlooked for promotion
- Repeated relationship failure
- Repeated weight loss failure

A third, and more subtle clue, is your speech. Specifically, the words you choose reveal the inner workings of your subconscious mind. Like:

- "It's dangerous to_____…"
- "It's risky to_____…"
- "I can't ever seem to_____…"
- "Life is always _____…"

> Any time you make a "blanket" statement; such as "things are always this way", this is a clue to your beliefs, or possibly a statement of a belief you hold to be true – a *fixed* belief.

What does any good detective do with clues? Solve the mystery! And that is what you will feel like as you go through our exercise, a really good and effective detective who solves your personal mysteries and opens your life to greater abundance of all that you want.

Types of beliefs

There are two primary types of beliefs – *simple* and the previously mentioned, *fixed*. Simple beliefs are more easily identified and can be changed with a little effort. If, for example, a friend of yours mentions he believes that *money is the root of all evil,* and that has always been one of your conscious, or unconscious, beliefs as well; your mind can flash a red flag that says "wait a minute, is that true?" As you reconsider this belief, compare it with recently gained insight like "money can be a valuable and useful tool to accomplish great good"; and "without financial capability the ability to help others is severely limited;" and "not everybody with money misuses it"... With the new possibilities you can then easily *change your mind* and replace a previously limiting belief with one that is more empowering and useful.

Fixed beliefs, on the other hand, are far more challenging to identify and replace! These are the beliefs your ego holds near and dear to protect you from perceived threats to your existence. They are a survival mechanism. As mentioned before, some are valuable and useful to keep, like *if I stand in front of an oncoming freight train, I could be killed or seriously injured.* Others, like *committed relationships always bring pain and loss of freedom,* can cause huge obstacles to the person trying to attract and stay in a love partnership. The latter are the beliefs this exercise seeks to identify and replace. Evaluating your results, patterns and speech are the clues you will use as you answer the questions in the Belief Change Exercise (BCE).

Why Transform a Belief?

Once you discover a *fixed* or *limiting* belief, why change it? Why not just continue to accept it and build your life around it?

The simple answer is either discomfort or personal growth or both.

If you are truly satisfied and content with your life as it is - relationships, health, wealth and their wide variety of scenarios - you seek this process for personal and spiritual growth. Actively redefining your belief system shifts your attitude, your perspective and ultimately your thoughts and behaviors which changes your life circumstances, conditions and relations.

Discomfort is feedback from your soul that something is not *right*, in *natural* or *perfect order* and *requires your attention.* Rather than respond, our unprepared, typical reaction is to ignore or bury the signal. A better response is to trace the feeling to its source, possibly a belief, then transform or replace it according to present day knowledge, skills and abilities. "Signal tracing" is the skill you will develop as you work through the BCE.

Now, let's develop those skills and solve the mystery!

Note:

An *incongruent* fixed belief acts like a powerful *repelling magnet*[9] – it is the opposite polarity of what you want – in the New Thought realm[10], "like attracts like"[1]; therefore, it pushes away and blocks any conflicting data or truths that might show up to disprove it. One compelling reason to work through the Belief Change Exercise is to clear your personal energy field of beliefs that repel what you want and align with empowering beliefs so that you can *attract your request(s)*!

Chapter 2

Belief Change Exercise

Simple BELIEF Change Exercise

IDENTIFY

the area where beliefs may be holding you back.

FIND

as many as possible of the negative or limiting beliefs that you might have in that area.

EVALUATE

The most important beliefs to address first.

HANDLE

Reduce the power of the belief by examining its effect on your life, and reevaluating its usefulness.

The goal of a redesigned, empowering belief system is habitual constructive and enjoyable actions – constantly under scrutiny as additional layers reveal and peel! Living intentionally!

Success Factors

As with any endeavor there are many critical and important aspects as outlined in the chapter titled *"The Dark Side"*; the most important success factors, however, for the BCE's effectiveness are your *willingness* and *persistence*. With these, the rest will fall into place.

Daily I receive <u>sincere</u> *get* _____ *quick scheme* offerings – fill in the blank with anything from *beautiful; younger; love; or rich* categories. Why? Because our human nature is looking for the *easy way* to get what we want, *effort* to achieve that goal is unpopular. Have you noticed the multiple forms of escapism many people choose to avoid confronting and resolving their problems, challenges and opportunities? Drugs, food, alcohol, sex, work, television, video games… just to name a few of the multitude of socially unacceptable and acceptable *temporary feel good* escapes.

Yet, instinctively we understand that most things worthwhile require effort. Certainly we can agree that most normal, healthy infants ultimately learn to walk. How many babies have you observed simply making up their mind to walk and in an instant, walking? How many babies have you observed struggle to master the skill: standing, falling, stepping, falling… over and over again, typically with a lot of encouragement and support through their skill development process. Why do we expect or wish for *different* when it comes to our important personal and emotion-laden goals?

Your willingness to apply knowledge to action is the only truly effective way to produce lasting, meaningful feel *great* results. *Get something for nothing schemes* may produce temporary results; typically, however, the problem they are meant to solve resurfaces because it surfaced in the first place for you to acknowledge, appreciate and resolve it! The problem serves your greater good and will not go away permanently until its purpose is satisfied. Then, you will absolutely feel *great*.

Therefore, to be a successful BCE participant there are some useful viewpoints that can assist your success:

- Everything in your life experience has value and its purpose is to bring you closer to fulfilling your destiny – your *greater good*.
- Facing and resolving emotional drama moves you step-by-step toward peace, meaning and fulfillment.
- What might seem like a huge amount of effort, when viewed as a *labor of love* for yourself and others around you, reinforces benefits.

Whether willing, able to embrace these viewpoints and persist – or not - there are times when tackling something alone can feel too daunting. So, if you intend to work through the BCE, yet recognize that it may be difficult for you to get through it by yourself, please consider exploring the Belief Change Facilitation program outlined in the *"What's Next"* chapter of this book or online at **www.beliefchangebook.com**. Many, if not all, of the most successful people in any given field succeeded with the help of a trained coach; this activity is no different. You may be an ideal candidate to benefit from participation in this program.

If you are willing, focused and determined then you will likely benefit from the BCE in the privacy and comfort of your very own space. Your confidence and skill mastery will grow as you work through each step.

The Belief Change Exercise and Its Theory

Following is the procedure, in its entirety. Each step correlates to a chapter in this workbook that contains instructions and theory - explanations of what to do and why.

Once you begin the exercise you may wish to use the version that contains only the steps, the exercise forms in the Appendix at the back of the book, which you can photocopy and write on as you do each step or the forms accessible online for printing at www. beliefchangebook.com. They contain the steps alone, with instructions, but no theory.

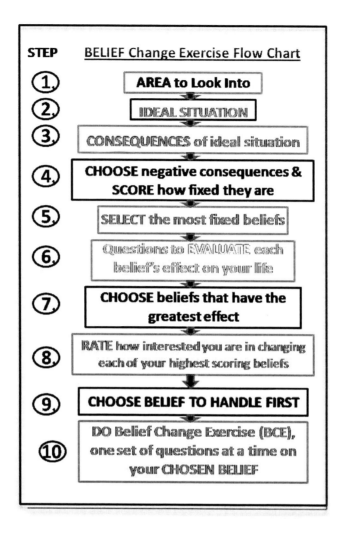

So how are you going to find limiting beliefs to work the exercise on if the key characteristic is that you totally believe they are true?

The simple answer is, by diligently working through the next 10 chapters, one step at a time. They walk you through our process of focusing in on the most difficult areas of your life or those you most want to improve. Initially you choose from among many possible discovered beliefs, one belief that is significantly limiting or blocking your success in the area you targeted to explore first. Note that working on and changing that first belief chosen is only the beginning. We encourage you to repeat the BCE, at a later time, on other beliefs surfaced but not selected this round.

Other beliefs that show up while you are doing the exercise, but are not quite so interesting as your initial selection, may well be the next to deal with once the first one is complete.

Considering the storage size of your mind's "databank" of beliefs, it is normal to have a number of these kinds of beliefs surface and many that would benefit from the BCE but obviously we begin and persist with the strongest and most relevant one. It's like plucking weeds from a beautiful garden, one weed or one clump at a time.

One of the best things about this exercise is that often, dealing with one or two "hot" beliefs can deactivate a lot of lesser beliefs attached to it – the whole "clump" loses its power.

Once you have chosen the first belief to address, you will answer questions that cause you to re-evaluate that one belief in relation to your current life. You should gain much greater understanding and awareness of how it has affected you: your happiness, success, etc.

Because this exercise is analogous to *peeling the onion*, as you work through it, discovery of a deeper belief can happen. Write it down for your next BCE (Belief Change Exercise) application then continue working on the belief you began.

Discovering a belief like this is a bonus – to address it you will be able to start at Step 4 (rating how fixed it is) and go on from there. Or even, if it is seriously over the top interesting, start at Step 10!

For the most powerful and effective BCE results, it is important to work each *layer* through to completion rather than stopping part way through and beginning the next belief.

> **Note:** If you work with an experienced Belief Change Facilitator, they might switch you onto working on a deeper belief. However, as you face up to these "demons" on your own, <u>it is more effective</u> to drain all the energy out of the one you started on before tackling the next.

We suggest that you study the preparatory chapters, including the Disclaimer as well as Chapter 3, *The Dark Side,* and Chapter 4, *Sharing Your Insights and Benefits*, before beginning the exercise.

The purpose of steps 1 - 9 of the BCE is to make sure that you have the best chance possible of identifying the most effective belief to address with Step 10.

Be aware that although there are other ways to find beliefs and remove them, and many other systems for doing so, and although we do encourage The Belief Change Facilitation support system, this Belief Change Exercise book has been designed to be a *Do-It-Yourself* application. Our goal throughout has been to make the BCE as simple and easy yet thorough and concise as possible for those who decide this journey is for them.

And on that note, if you are tempted to just skip ahead and start the exercise, please do remember to read the next chapter (3) – a much more thorough 'warnings' section!

Chapter 3

"THE DARK SIDE"

Who may not be able to benefit from the Belief Change Exercise

Preparation

- well fed – preferably protein
- **well rested – not tired**
- no medication – if possible
- **no alcohol – for about a day before**

As with all human endeavors, there are always going to be some people who will do beautifully at the activity; they will sail through and have extraordinary results. For others it will be a struggle, *or* they will not even attempt it, *or* will try and give up.

Because these are individual situations that we cannot predict, we include a few notes on what may make it difficult for someone to maintain a level of concentration and dedication that brings success and change from applying this exercise.

The foremost thing is to make sure you have read and understood the disclaimer at the beginning of the book right before the introduction.

Additionally, you want to do these exercises on your own *only* if you feel totally comfortable about investigating your past activities and choices.

Living your life in an environment where you are being "put down" or "made less of" on a regular basis can undo or seriously detract from your benefits from the Belief Change System. Being subjected to constant criticism and blaming usually has the effect of wiping out any positive changes gained. It is wise to end this type of experience, if possible, or at least avoid the source of such negativity, otherwise you may find yourself alternately improving then taking a dive, on and on. Barbara De Angelis[11] has written excellent books on "toxic" people which can add to your understanding if you are in this type of situation. There are ways to handle these situations, but that is the subject of a different program. For further information see website details at the end of the book.

If you have done a lot of personal growth work or seminars of other kinds, such as rebirthing, transcendental meditation or belief exercises offered by other personal development cultures; and if those kinds of procedures are mixed with this one, or done during the same time period, confusion can arise and results may be less than can be achieved when applying the BCE exactly as laid down.

A person who lives their life in a state of frequently judging or criticizing others, making people and life wrong and blaming others for things that happen to them, complaining, justifying their failures and mistakes rather than taking responsibility for their circumstances and conditions then doing something to improve or correct them may have considerable trouble doing the BCE. As will the perpetual victim who wallows in that state; in fact, these people may dismiss any value to the book and the exercise as well as make it wrong because their beliefs may not allow them to perceive that they CAN change their life. If, however, they do face up and complete the exercise they are likely to produce considerable changes providing they do it honestly.

There is no way to control how anyone will use any exercise or system presented in a publication or whether they will follow it correctly, and we of course will accept no liability or responsibility whatsoever for any lack of results, or negative consequences that may arise from applying this Belief Change Exercise. It is entirely your decision.

The information above is to help readers make a judgment as to whether this exercise is as likely to work for them as it does consistently with people in a good state to begin with, who work the exercises. If you are interested in doing the Belief Change Exercise but feel you need help, it is possible to join a facilitation program to help get through the exercises. Refer to the information in the "What's Next" chapter at the end of this book or online at www.beliefchangebook.com..

Chapter 4

SHARING YOUR INSIGHTS AND BENEFITS

This chapter covers a few things you need to be aware of when you discuss what you find and learn doing the exercises, or sharing your experiences and insights with others.

Typically, in a workshop, a success factor is a facilitator trained in *ability development* and *enhancement processes*. They facilitate their clients' new insights and skill development. They are thoroughly familiar with the basics and ground rules of what supports success working each step of the exercise and what does not.

A trained facilitator is aware that the greatest error that can be made is to "put down", make wrong, judge, or belittle the client or their issues, viewpoints and discoveries. It is their objective and responsibility to create a safe environment for revelation, understanding and growth. Criteria and technique is a primary focus for their certification process and facilitator code of ethics.

Even simply stating an opinion on what the client communicates violates the facilitation activity *code* because it diminishes or even destroys the safety of the client/facilitator relationship. "Making wrong" someone's viewpoints, opinions, or experiences is the most extreme violation of the guidelines for success in a facilitator/client situation, but even the mild version – stating opinions – is detrimental to the effectiveness of this type of exercise. Valuable information about the "make wrong" phenomena can be found in Eckhart Tolle's[12] books and publications

Because you are doing this on your own, facilitator conduct would not normally be a potential problem. Friends and family members are typically untrained in creating a safe environment criteria and techniques.

What might become a problem for you is if you decide you want to share your findings, insights and successes with another or others, and those others do not understand fundamental rules of safe communication.

We prefer that you do not lose your benefits and gains by having them *put down* or *made wrong* by someone who does not understand the importance of a "safe space" for you to release your past problems, upsets, mistakes and misjudgments – to "unburden" yourself.

The last thing you need to hear when you open up and share your innermost thoughts and feelings are comments like "That's crazy or a waste of time, there's nothing wrong with you, why are you bothering with that BS?" or "Oh, I always knew you did that, I've been trying to tell you for years, why didn't you listen to me and save yourself the price of the book?"

Doing this exercise is entirely your choice, and we offer it knowing we have no control at all over whether you follow the guidelines that increase the likelihood of its success.

The same applies to your choice to share your exercise results and insights with another: it is your responsibility to make quite sure that a recipient of your confidences in this matter is a SAFE confidant! That they will not betray your confidences, will not in any way judge, make wrong or give advice about the exercise or what shows up for you while working the exercise. In fact, it works best if you prepare them beforehand to keep their face neutral but interested, their opinions to themselves, and to only say, "I got it", "I understand", or "Great!" after you have shared what you experienced.

If you make an error in judgment on this and your confidant DOES break the rules, the one thing we can guarantee is you will have a learning experience! But it will also give you an insight into who in your life is supportive of your personal expansion and improvement. The value of a safe person with whom to communicate will be very clear.

If this happens it can be an indication of a hidden negative intent towards you, or at very best, a degree of ignorance of the fundamentals of intimacy and friendship.

And it can also point to an area to explore for a belief that people you trust seem to betray that trust. There are many people we have encountered while doing this work who have entrenched beliefs to the effect that "If you trust people they will eventually betray you" and similar wordings.

If this should happen you might well want to apply the Belief Change Exercise to this situation!

Chapter 5

Belief Change Exercise (BCE) Step 1

Identify an area of your life in which to look for limiting beliefs.

**Belief Change
Exercise
Step 1**
CHOOSE an area of
your life you would
like to improve
(this could be an area of
CONSTANT PROBLEMS
or DIFFICULTY)

The following list is a cross-section of common areas of life that you might have an interest in improving. They are areas of life that past workshop participants have effectively worked through the process to improve, enhance or unblock.

- Abilities
- Money and Wealth
- Physical Well-being and Health
- Relationships, including Family, Children, & Business relationships

- Lifestyle
- Business
- Work or Career
- Team or Group Co-operation
- Success and Goal Achievement
- Personal Growth
- Self Esteem and Self Confidence
- Spirituality
- Education and Learning
- Satisfaction and Fulfillment
- Adaptability and Flexibility
- Excitement
- Motivation and Passion
- Age and Aging
- Appearance and image
- Order and managing disorder
- Commitment and keeping agreements
- Responsibility and accountability
- Delegation
- Leadership
- Competence and effectiveness
- Friends
- Community
- Nutrition
- Weight or size
- Correcting or handling mistakes
- Wisdom and maturity
- Organization and systems

- Possessions
- Intelligence and mental abilities
- Love
- Sex life and sexual well-being
- Romance
- Power
- Persistence & follow-through
- Ability to market and sell
- Acceptance and belonging
- Trust of self & others
- Time management & time agreements
- Achieving emotional balance & healthy emotional expression
- Ability to experience and express feelings
- Production & Productivity
- Creativity
- Happiness
- Ability to change with the times
- Ability to learn from your mistakes
- Ability to effectively change and improve your life
- Contribution to society
- Stress and reactions to stress
- Ability to face up to unpleasant realities

These are not the only possibilities; we include them solely for your consideration and to engage your ego's contribution. For the first step, you will select an area from the list or choose from your personal experience. It is critical to identify only *one*, early testing of the procedure as a "Do-It-Yourself" exercise proved that attempts to resolve an entire lifetime in one session was ineffective! Typically, dozens of negative beliefs surface and working through them all at once can become overwhelming, confusing and challenging.

Interest is the primary factor for selecting which area to work first. If relationships present your biggest life challenges but you are not ready to confront it, let it go until you are. Focus on something you can face; an area you think you can effectively address.

On the other hand, if your stuck area and total focus is on one that feels too difficult to work through, for example self-esteem and self-confidence, but no other area seems interesting to you, then you might want to tackle it anyway. Examine one piece at a time and see how it goes. Each small win accumulates and over time the huge obstacle dissolves.

As you work through the exercise, your priorities are likely to change. When things shift for the better in the area you are addressing as you go through the exercise, you may want to enjoy that change for a few days and let it stabilize. This provides you an opportunity to "road test" the belief, to see if it is still influencing you in your life, and if it needs any further work. Then either come back to the exercise and work through it some more, if the belief is still interesting, or pick another from your Step 8 list (high interest, highlighted) and begin the Step 10 questions on it.

Step 1 Action:

Choose and record the area you want to work.

When complete, move on to Step 2.

Chapter 6

Belief Change Exercise (BCE) Step 2

Describe the Ideal Situation for your chosen area

**Belief Change
Exercise
Step 2**

**LIST how you would
like
your life to be in that
area
IDEAL SITUATION**

What does describing your ideal situation have to do with beliefs?

Quote from the Cheshire Cat in *Alice in Wonderland*:

"If you don't know where you are going, any road will get you there."[12]

Similarly, for this exercise to help you discover your limiting beliefs you must first imagine how your life would be if you did not have any beliefs holding you back in that area – your ideal situation.

Limiting beliefs are often those sneaky negative thoughts that show up when you imagine living an ideal aspect of life. They are mind chatter about all the bad that could happen when the ideal becomes real. Sometimes these are not obvious because they appear to protect you in some way.

For example, if you envision an abundance of money and the ability to choose your own lifestyle, the sneaky little thought that might show up is *"I will be too busy managing my money to enjoy my lifestyle."* Or, *"If I'm rich no one will like me any more except to get money from me."* Or,… Until you recognize and evaluate this mind chatter for potential limitations or barriers it can operate as an anchor preventing you moving toward your goal.

Some examples of descriptions of an ideal situation in the area of life for someone picking "Abilities" might include:
- "fluently speak a foreign language"
- "I can bench press 300 lbs"
- "I am fast, smart and capable"
- "I can easily make millions of dollars doing what I love" …

Using a form from the Appendix in the back of this book vividly describe your vision of the ideal situation in your target area. Keep the description reasonably short, in a list format, as above; you want one key idea clearly described.

One technique for describing your ideal is to identify what you *no longer want to experience* in your chosen area and then write down the *opposite* – the opposite is what you *do want*. Another technique is to describe *role models* or *successes*.

Step 2 Action:

Describe **your chosen area's ideal situation clearly and exactly in the form of a list.**

The next step helps you identify any subconscious negative consequences perceived as a direct or indirect result of ideal situation manifestation.

Chapter 7

Belief Change Exercise (BCE) Step 3

List Possible Consequences of Achieving Your Ideal Situation

**Belief Change
Exercise
Step 3**

**LIST possible
consequences,
positive & negative,
If you had already
achieved your
IDEAL SITUATION
*underline negative ones***

Now, imagine your ideal situation. What will your life be like? What will be different? What makes your heart sing when you imagine it becoming reality in your life? On your form from the back of this book or the **www.beliefchangebook.com** website, make a list of as many possible consequences or potential differences as you can imagine.

In other words, if you get what you want or achieve your ideal situation, what might be the results of doing so?

Remain alert for any thoughts that show up about the negative or down side of achieving your ideals – if you believe or even think there are potential negative consequences from reaching your goals and dreams, this could lead to a belief that limits, blocks or slows your achieving the ideal situation you desire.

One format for doing this is to preface your ideal situation statement with the words "**if I were…**", "**if I had...**", "**if I did…**". Or whatever makes it into a sensible sentence. For example:

- *"If I were* a well respected writer I would influence others for the good."
- *"If I were* a well-respected writer I could help to change the world."
- *"If I were* a well-respected writer, yet wrote something unpopular, critics might attack me and make my life miserable."
- *"If I were* a well-respected writer, yet wrote something controversial, vested interests might try to silence me."

Initially you can expect the positives to show up; write them down. Remain alert for the downside or negative possibilities to show up. They can show up as a feeling of discomfort or dread, or a sense of gloom and uncertainty. That is a probable sign a limiting belief is lurking in the background.

When you think of or consider others that you observe or witness of others living your ideal, what comes to mind? It is possible you have a belief that what happened to them could happen to you.

Many of you might expect to think about your ideal situation and feel only happy, excited, uplifted and motivated. That is often not true, because if there were nothing in the way – no negative feelings about achieving your ideal situation – odds are you would already have it and wouldn't have chosen this area to address.

So, when thinking about your ideal situation, notice any interruptions to the pleasant feelings. The unpleasant thoughts likely indicate a buried belief; write the thoughts down. Limiting beliefs are the ones that make you unwilling to go after the ideal situation.

While there will be many positive feelings associated with the ideal situation, or you wouldn't even be interested in achieving it, for the BCE we are only going to work with the negative ones. Positive beliefs are the fuel that powers you onward. Usually they only need strengthening by deactivating negative beliefs that detract from their becoming reality.

As you write your lists of consequences (and it could be quite long if you have a lot of ideal situations listed in step 2) **mark a "–" (minus sign) beside the negative consequences and a "+" (plus sign) beside the positive ones**.
Then **<u>underline all the negative or limiting ones</u>**.

It is optional whether you write in **"the consequences would be…"** or not. Use the sheet labeled "Step 3" provided in the appendix or print the Step 3 form found on the website www.beliefchangebook.com. The following are some examples of consequence statements, with their labels, positive and negative.

Example 1: *Wealth*

If I were affluent and prospering (the consequences or result would be) I could help a lot of people +

If I were affluent and prospering … I could do anything I wanted +

If I were affluent and prospering everyone would depend on me to support them –

If I were affluent and prospering I would have to pay way too much   taxes –

If I were affluent and prospering I would feel much happier than I am now +

If I were affluent and prospering people wouldn't like me for myself –

If I were affluent and prospering I'd have nothing left to learn –

If I were affluent and prospering I might lose my spirituality –

If I were affluent and prospering my kids would never learn how to become tough enough to handle adversity –

If I were affluent and prospering I'd never know whether people cared about me or the money –

If I were affluent and prospering I might become really obnoxious to people who aren't –

If I had consistent passive income I wouldn't have to be dependent on a job anymore +

If I had consistent passive income I might get really lazy –

If I had consistent passive income I might lose my sense of purpose –

If I had consistent passive income my kids might never learn how to make money and get wealthy themselves –

If I had consistent passive income I'd get complacent and lose my drive –

Example 2: *Romance*

If I were in a committed romantic relationship I would probably get   bored –

If I were in a committed romantic relationship I would feel very secure and happily ecstatic +

If I were in a committed romantic relationship I might let my partner down –

If I were in a committed romantic relationship I might lose my freedom –

If I were in a committed romantic relationship we'd lose interest in sex pretty quickly –

If I were in a committed romantic relationship I would have a great companion to share my time with +

If I were in a committed romantic relationship I might not be able to go out with my friends anymore –

As you work through this part of the exercise, the objective is to end up with enough negative consequences (which are potential beliefs to handle) that you can then work through them, gradually eliminate the less significant ones and pick out the most useful to handle.

Step 3 Action:

Using the Step 3 page from the Appendix or the website www.beliefchangebook.com, *list* **all possible consequences,** *designate* **them "+" or "–" and** *underline* **all the negative ones.**

This step produces the list you will be working on through the remainder of the steps. Some people might have just a few, others can end up with pages; Steps 4 – 9 then narrow it down eventually to the first one to start the exercise on.

Chapter 8

Belief Change Exercise (BCE) Step 4

Rate How Fixed Each Belief Is

Belief Change Exercise Step 4

SCORE each of the *negative underlined* **Consequences** from 0-10 Depending on how fixed it is

You now have a list of possible negative beliefs – the possible consequences you have outlined above – which we will continue to work on through to Step 9.

> You might ask at this point what to do with the positive beliefs – the ideal situation you envisioned. You do nothing more with them for the purpose of the BCE. However, we recommend writing the positive ones on a poster board, with colored pens and hanging it on the wall to remind you of how you *want* your life to look!

Step 4 is about differentiation – which potential beliefs are relevant and holding you back, which ones are insignificant or less important right now? To what degree are they blocking your success? How strongly does this idea have a hold on you?

Why waste your time evaluating and handling potential beliefs that, when complete, are unlikely to produce a shift that moves you closer to your ideal situation? How much more powerful is this exercise when it reveals the more foundational beliefs upon which the less significant ones are built? Which one might be the first belief that starts to pull the plug on many others?

Just a warning – at this early stage in the exercise you may start to see already which beliefs are "hotter", and even pick one that seems like "it". Be careful not to turn this into a search for the "Holy Grail of Beliefs"! We are not hunting for a magical one belief to handle that solves all the problems of the universe, we are just narrowing the choices to a few from which we can choose the most interesting to start on.

The first nine steps of the BCE act like the focus aperture of a laser beam. They continue to narrow down the list using the process of elimination, sifting out the less powerful and less relevant ones. Finally focusing in on the possible beliefs that fit the criteria of being strongly fixed and limiting so that the first one you tackle in Step 10, when you turn on the metaphoric *laser beam* is most likely to produce the maximum change.

In Step 4, you will rate each underlined possible belief, from "0 – 10", as to how fixed, real or *"cast in concrete"* it is.

If you feel the possible belief is an incontrovertible fact of life; in fact, you aren't really sure it could even be called a belief because it "really is true", it gets a "9" or a "10"!

Not true, i.e., you don't believe it at all, is a "0".

If you feel you would have no trouble changing your mind about it, you might rate it a "1" or a "2".

"5" is a "maybe"; it seems to be true but you would be able to change your mind about it without much effort.

You might rate it "6" if you believe it isn't true but you don't think you can change it by just deciding it isn't true.

Exact ratings are not crucial. *Close* is good enough for differentiation between the "heavy-duty" beliefs that can ruin an area of your life and less significant ones that can piggyback on the "hot" ones.

The ideal phenomena we want you to experience after applying Step 10, the Belief Change Exercise (which is the actual handling step for your target belief) is that many of the other beliefs on the Consequences List collapse or become unfixed as well. Similar to pulling a support beam from a wall and a big chunk of the house collapses. It doesn't happen in every case but it's a great bonus when it does!

Step 4 Action:

Working with your Consequences List from Step 3 *rate* **each underlined, negative possible consequence from "0 – 10" as described.** Ask yourself, "How true, certain or real is this possible consequence?" and grade it accordingly.

Example of how this might look, using the Consequences List from Step 3, subject: Wealth. For simplicity we have deleted the positive consequences, but on your own list they will be mixed together when you first make your Step 3 list.

If I were affluent and prospering everyone would depend on me to support them – **8**

If I were affluent and prospering I would have to pay way too much taxes – **7**

If I were affluent and prospering people wouldn't like me for myself – **9**

If I were affluent and prospering I'd have nothing left to learn – **7**

If I were affluent and prospering I might lose my spirituality – **6**

If I were affluent and prospering my kids would never learn how to become tough enough to handle adversity – **6**

If I were affluent and prospering I'd never know whether people cared about me or the money – **8**

If I were affluent and prospering I might become really obnoxious to people who aren't – **7**

If I had consistent passive income I might get really lazy – **7**

If I had consistent passive income I might lose my sense of purpose – **9**

If I had consistent passive income my kids might never learn how to make money and get wealthy themselves – **4**

If I had consistent passive income I'd get complacent and lose my drive – **7**

6 – is to answer 7 questions about each belief remaining on the list after Step 5.

Too many potential beliefs to evaluate this way could be quite tedious for some people and defeat the purpose of the exercise – which does involve keeping your interest and making progress, not struggling to cover every tiny possible belief just in case you miss something.

And as you are only going to end up with one to start with, there's no point doing the detailed evaluation involved in this next step on lukewarm possible beliefs and possibly getting overwhelmed by evaluating so many.

Example of Step 5, using the consequences already scored in the Step 4 example. On this particular example we end up with 8 beliefs to take through the next step.

If I were affluent and prospering everyone would depend on me to support them – **8** *

If I were affluent and prospering I would have to pay way too much taxes – **7** *

If I were affluent and prospering people wouldn't like me for myself – **9** *

If I were affluent and prospering I'd have nothing left to learn – **7** *

If I were affluent and prospering I might lose my spirituality – **6**

If I were affluent and prospering my kids would never learn how to become tough enough to handle adversity – **5**

If I were affluent and prospering I'd never know whether people cared about me or the money – **8** *

If I were affluent and prospering I might become really obnoxious to people who aren't – **7** *

If I had consistent passive income I might get really lazy – **7** *

If I had consistent passive income I might lose my sense of purpose – **9** *

If I had consistent passive income my kids might never learn how to make money and get wealthy themselves – **4**

If I had consistent passive income I'd get complacent and lose my drive – **7** *

> **Note:** As you move through these steps, if the list gets a little confusing – and it may get a LOT confusing as you continue to write various ratings on each belief – you might want to either write out your highest scoring (most fixed) negative beliefs on a new sheet of paper, or transfer them now to the "Belief Change Exercise Worksheet" you'll find at the back of the book. Additionally, if a new negative possibility comes to mind: add, underline and score it.

Chapter 9

Belief Change Exercise (BCE) Step 5

Identify The Most Fixed of The Negative Beliefs

Belief Change Exercise Step 5

MARK with an *

the BELIEFS

that scored the

HIGHEST

Usually

10's, 9.s, 8's, 7's

Include 6's if there aren't

many above 7

Step 5 is an extension of Step 4; you are still narrowing your focus. This simple step identifies the top scoring beliefs by putting an asterisk beside them.

But there are a few things that can be a little confusing about which are highest scoring. For example, you might have 2 or 3 "10s" but your next highest scoring ones are only

"5s" and you have 10 or 12 of them. It is unlikely that any of the "5s" will be the one you start on first, so you may want to leave them out and continue on with a small list.

If you have a large number of "10s" and a large number of "9s", it might be unwise to exclude the "9s" just because you have so many. It is possible one of them might be the best beginning belief so leaving out the 9s would miss that one.

One reason for selecting only the top ranking beliefs is simply the amount of time it would take to evaluate all of them in the later Step 6. However, your list will be valuable to you in the future. You may see that the belief you selected is related to other high-scoring limiting beliefs or you might want to complete the exercise on those that remain an issue for you at a future time.

Step 5 Action:

Place an asterisk * next to the top scoring, underlined, limiting beliefs. Start by marking all with the highest score, then the next highest, etc. For your first time through the BCE on this step, try to select a reasonable number of possible beliefs which you will then evaluate further on Step 6.

The reason it is best not to end up with too large a number on your list after this step is that your next action – Step 6 – is to answer 7 questions about each belief remaining on the list after Step 5.

Too many potential beliefs to evaluate this way could be quite tedious for some people and defeat the purpose of the exercise – which does involve keeping your interest and making progress, not struggling to cover every tiny possible belief just in case you miss something.

And as you are only going to end up with one to start with, there's no point doing the detailed evaluation involved in this next step on lukewarm possible beliefs and possibly getting overwhelmed by evaluating so many.

Example of Step 5, using the consequences already scored in the Step 4 example. On this particular example we end up with 8 beliefs to take through the next step.

If I were affluent and prospering everyone would depend on me to support them – **8** *

If I were affluent and prospering I would have to pay way too much taxes – **7** *

If I were affluent and prospering people wouldn't like me for myself – **9** *

If I were affluent and prospering I'd have nothing left to learn – **7** *

If I were affluent and prospering I might lose my spirituality – **6**

If I were affluent and prospering my kids would never learn how to become tough enough to handle adversity – **5**

If I were affluent and prospering I'd never know whether people cared about me or the money – **8** *

If I were affluent and prospering I might become really obnoxious to people who aren't – **7** *

If I had consistent passive income I might get really lazy – **7** *

If I had consistent passive income I might lose my sense of purpose – **9** *

If I had consistent passive income my kids might never learn how to make money and get wealthy themselves – **4**

If I had consistent passive income I'd get complacent and lose my drive – **7** *

Chapter 10

Belief Change Exercise (BCE) Step 6

Determine Impact of Your Fixed Beliefs On Your Life

Belief Change Exercise Step 6

On each high scoring

* BELIEF

answer the 7 questions about its effect on your life

MARK each "YES" answer with a **/** mark

(**|||| ||** is the highest possible score)

This step establishes how much each belief has affected your life, happiness and general well-being up to this point. It consists of 7 questions, answerable by a "yes" or a "no", to further discern the power and effect of each of your previously underlined and asterisked beliefs.

Note: these questions can be VERY uncomfortable and stressful to consider – it is not easy to admit you sometimes use obviously ineffective solutions to your problems! However, if you can be honest with yourself, the results will overpower any embarrassment you experience completing Step 6.

Step 6 Action:

Considering the first of your asterisked beliefs, answer the following 7 questions about it. Then repeat for each asterisked belief on your Consequences list.

On each underlined and asterisked belief with a "yes" answer to one of the 7 questions, place a "slash" mark next to it. For a "no" answer, you leave it unmarked. The greatest number of slash marks you can end up with on each belief is 7 – all "yes" answers.

The first question, "**Does this belief _fill in the blank_ hold you back from doing what you want or making progress towards your goals?**" addresses one of the main characteristics of a truly fixed belief – it blocks you. It slows you down or prevents you from achievement. Does this belief warn you of all that will go wrong when this belief manifests? Is there a little voice reminding you of all the consequences that you won't like when you reach your goal? Has this belief prevented you from living your ideal situation?

Action: Mark the belief you are evaluating with a slash mark (/) beside it if it's a "yes" answer. For a "no" answer, leave it unmarked.

The second question, "**Does this belief _fill in the blank_ prevent you from facing up to an area of your life and dealing with it?**" addresses the aspect of denial. Are you using the belief in some way to avoid confronting and addressing very real issues in some part of your life? Are you using it to deny or push away reality?

For example, the kids run wild and ignore the rules of the home. The belief you had adopted is, "If I have fun-loving and happy kids I won't need to control them at all." This belief enables you to avoid the fact that their behavior is not helping them, you or anyone else and you don't feel you have to do anything to correct their behavior.

This belief stops you from sitting down with them and explaining how you feel about what they are doing, establishing boundaries and delivering consequences. It helps you avoid controlling their self-sabotaging and destructive behavior and teaching them responsibility and accountability. It keeps you from having to face their emotions and reactions if you do try to deal with it. And so on…

Action: Mark the belief you are evaluating with a slash mark (/) beside it if it's a "yes" answer. For a "no" answer, leave it unmarked.

The third question, **"Does this belief __*fill in the blank*__ seem to solve some problem area in your life?",** addresses the issue not from a denial viewpoint but from a perspective of "Does the belief seem to make the problems go away or vanish?"

For example, a person always has problems in their relationships with the opposite sex, and the belief they finally adopted might be "If I have a great intimate relationship with a woman she will find out about my unresolved issues and leave me."

And guess what? That "really works"! The behaviors the belief brings about now keep him from getting close to women. So here he is, the problem area has vanished, solved, because any woman he might get close to just somehow vanishes, leaves him! Chased away by his attitude. End of problem! But end of relationships too…

Action: Mark the belief you are evaluating with a slash mark (/) beside it if it's a "yes" answer. For a "no" answer, leave it unmarked.

The fourth question, **"Does this belief __*fill in the blank*__ seem to you to be so true that you can't imagine how your life would be if you didn't believe it or if you found out it wasn't true?"** actually readdresses some of what was covered in Step 4 and 5. How fixed is this belief?

The most difficult and limiting beliefs are the ones that seem like "the truth, the whole truth and nothing but the truth." Beliefs with this degree of fixedness are usually fundamental cornerstones of your whole system of beliefs. Exploring them can provide the deepest insight and have the greatest impact and benefit on your ability to fulfill your dreams!

Typically this will be a belief that is so engrained and deep-seated that it hinders or prevents you from being able in any way to evaluate the belief accurately. This is a belief that is so entwined with who you think you are that there is not enough separation between you and it for you to see that it might not be serving you in a positive way. This of course is exactly what you *must* do to overcome your limitations!

Action: Mark the belief you are evaluating with a slash mark (/) beside it if it's a "yes" answer. For a "no" answer, leave it unmarked.

Note that many beliefs that can be addressed with a lot of benefit still aren't in this extreme category; so don't worry if it's a "no" on this question. It's just a bonus if you manage to uncover one or more of these.

The Fifth Question, **"Does this belief ___*fill in the blank*___ seem to stop you from thinking logically and rationally about your target area of difficulty as well as working out how to handle it?**

One characteristic of a sabotaging belief is that it hinders one's ability to think logically about the subject. For example, a belief that *"If you have trust in people's honesty, then you will end up being cheated"* makes it extremely difficult for an individual to fully engage with people, family, co-workers, and partners. This person feels unsafe. Consequently, to protect himself from the consequences he expects, he adds into his thinking the certainty that he will be cheated. He further confuses the issue with elaborate and probably unnecessary precautions to prevent what he just *"KNOWS"* will be the outcome – they will cheat him somehow no matter what he does. He behaves in a way that predisposes him to the expected outcome; e.g., treating people abruptly, disrespectfully, or suspiciously. Self-fulfilling prophecy – he sets the stage for his belief to come true!

Action: Mark the belief you are evaluating with a slash mark (/) beside it if it's a "yes" answer. For a "no" answer, leave it unmarked.

The Sixth Question: **"Has this belief ___*fill in the blank*___ caused you to feel you are a little better than other people?"** is different from the previous questions. It addresses a deeper and more subtle aspect of the belief phenomena.

One aspect of a fixed belief is that it seems to help to justify us being the way we are – it justifies not changing. It can show up as a subtle feeling of righteousness and a sense of superiority over other people because *you know better than they*.

Let's use an example from Step 3, *"if I had passive income I might get lazy"*. How might a person use this belief to feel superior to others?

People who operate from this belief subconsciously sabotage their financial freedom. They might justify their results by showing how hard working *they* are and how they are too righteous to receive money unless it is earned through effort and struggle. They can use their belief to feel better than those who they categorize as "lazy and receiving money without working."

The truth is that in a healthy functional society without sabotage by people of ill intent, where people have free will and many choices there is abundance – *enough* for everybody! In such a society, people use their talents to create with passion not struggle, and welfare is limited to support through times of crisis, not a way of life. When a society allows opportunities for ethical passive income, the person who uses that leverage can live a fulfilling, meaningful life. Ethical passive income combined with meaningful contribution that may or may not include active income, enables personal and collective compassion, benevolence and achievement of destiny!

The person with a belief that makes passive income, or people enjoying passive income seem wrong, can gain satisfaction from feeling better than those who benefit from passive income. However, people holding this limiting belief will most likely never achieve financial freedom and feel dissatisfied as they struggle financially and to fulfill their dreams.

Action: Mark the belief you are evaluating with a slash mark (/) beside it if it's a "yes" answer. For a "no" answer, leave it unmarked.

The Seventh Question: **"Has this belief** _**fill in the blank**_ **had an effect of making other people feel put down or less than you?"** is similar to the last question but is the other aspect of feeling superior. With a belief like the passive income example, when you feel better than others they can subconsciously sense your attitude and feel put down, minimized or even unethical because they are apparently accepting money without going through a struggle to earn it. Your attitude can communicate wordlessly as well as by what you say on the subject.

Like the previous question, one of the most dangerously subtle aspects of this belief in action is a perpetual justification for lack of success. The belief functions as an excuse or rationalization for not succeeding without a lot of work and struggle. It makes the concept of having free time to do what you love, add value to the world etc, seem *wrong* as well as making wrong any people who are actually enjoying the luxuries of passive income.

An individual with this belief will tend to be critical of wealthy people and might call them lazy or suggest that they do not do work or add value to the world. Consequently, even if they are open to a different perspective, they will likely have trouble making friends and building relationships that could provide them insight and information to change their belief!

Action: Mark the belief you are evaluating with a slash mark (/) beside it if it's a "yes" answer. For a "no" answer, leave it unmarked

Although we exampled a belief around passive income to show how Questions 6 and 7 can be applied, beliefs about race, religion, gender, social class, nationality, age, body type, occupation etc (i.e. all the categories in Step 1) can all contain this aspect of helping one to feel superior and others inferior … the list is long.

By the end of Step 6 your Step 3 (Consequences List) beliefs will all be marked as positive "+" or negative "–"; the negatives will be underlined and scored for fixedness, asterisked and sifted down to the most impactful with between 0 and 7 slash marks beside them. You now know a little more about what motivates some of your behaviors and you have a "short list" out of what you started from. You are ready for Step 7!

Example of Step 6, using the highest scoring beliefs from Step 5. On the real list you make, the lower scoring beliefs NOT marked with an asterisk * will be on the list, you just won't do this step and any further ones on them.

If I were affluent and prospering everyone <u>would</u> depend on me to support them – **8**   *   ///// /

<u>*If I were* affluent and prospering I would have to pay way too much taxes</u> – **7**   *   ////

If I were affluent and prospering people wouldn't like me for myself – **9**   *   ///// //

<u>*If I were* affluent and prospering I'd have nothing left to learn</u> – **7**   *   ///

<u>*If I were* affluent and prospering I might lose my spirituality</u> – **6**

<u>*If I were* affluent and prospering my kids would never learn how to become tough enough to handle adversity</u> – **5**

<u>*If I were* affluent and prospering I'd never know whether people cared about me or the money</u> – **8**   *   ///// //

<u>*If I were* affluent and prospering I might become really obnoxious to people who aren't</u> – **7**   *   ///// /

<u>*If I had* consistent passive income I might get really lazy</u> –   **7**   *   ///// /

<u>*If I had* consistent passive income I might lose my sense of purpose</u> – **9**   *   /////

<u>*If I had* consistent passive income my kids might never learn how to make money and get wealthy themselves</u> –   **4**

<u>*If I had* consistent passive income I'd get complacent and lose my drive</u> –   **7**   *   /////

Chapter 11

Belief Change Exercise (BCE) Step 7

Create the "Hot List" – the beliefs with the most impact on your life.

**Belief Change
Exercise
Step 7**

**MARK with a
HIGHLIGHTER
your
highest scoring
BELIEFS
(usually 6 & 7's
but can include
4 & 5's)**

From your list begun in Step 3 you now select the highest scoring beliefs (out of a possible total of 7) from Step 6. This is an elimination process that fine-tunes your focus to the "juicy" ones.

Obviously, any beliefs that tally 7 out of 7 slash marks are on your "hot list." So are the ones with 6. Mark these with a highlighter. If your highest tallies are 4s and 5s, mark those with a highlighter.

Completing Step 6 increased your understanding of each belief you evaluated. And now you leave out the ones that have not been much of a barrier or problem in your life. If you still have a very large list by this stage, just be aware that you might get a little overwhelmed when making your final choice of the one to work with first.

Step 7 narrows your choices further to the beliefs that have most impact on your life, and by this point you are probably getting a clearer idea of which those are.

Remember, this exercise can be repeated as many times as you wish – you do not have to do it *all* in one sitting!

That being said, your final selection must be extensive enough for you to evaluate the one you are going to work on first. *If* you only have a couple with 7 slashes on your list, for this step include your "6's" and maybe "5's" as well. A belief with 4 or 5 slash marks becomes significant if you have none with 6 or 7.

Step 7 Action:

Highlight the highest scoring of the beliefs on your list that you just evaluated in Step 6. Select the highest scoring beliefs from Step 6 and mark each one with a highlighter, starting with the highest scores and working down.

At the end of this step you have a fine-tuned list from the one you began back in Step 3. It typically might have anywhere from 5 to 30 highlighted negative beliefs.

Step 7 example: We end up with 7 of the asterisked beliefs highlighted, each with 5 slashes or above. You could include the one with 4 slashes – that still indicates that one has had some impact on your life.

If I were affluent and prospering everyone would depend on me to support them – **8** * ///// /

If I were affluent and prospering I would have to pay way too much taxes – **7** * ////

If I were affluent and prospering people wouldn't like me for myself – **9** * ///// //

If I were affluent and prospering I'd have nothing left to learn – **7** * ///

If I were affluent and prospering I might lose my spirituality – **6**

If I had were affluent and prospering my kids would never learn how to become tough enough to handle adversity – **5**

If I were affluent and prospering I'd never know whether people cared about me or the money – **8** * ///// //

If I were affluent and prospering I might become really obnoxious to people who aren't – **7** * ///// /

If I had consistent passive income I might get really lazy – **7** * ///// /

If I had consistent passive income I might lose my sense of purpose – **9** * /////

I f I had consistent passive income my kids might never learn how to make money and get wealthy themselves – **4**

If I had consistent passive income I'd get complacent and lose my drive – **7** * /////

IMPORTANT NOTE: At some point after the Step 6 evaluation, or even before, it may become clear to you which belief you want to work on first, or maybe you definitely know the 2 or 3 that your final choice will be made from. That is OK, and it may mean you have naturally already done Steps 8 and 9 — choosing which ones you'd most urgently like to change and picking the one to start with.

If that happens, you do not have to hold yourself up wading through these steps before you start Step 10 on your chosen belief.

You can just circle your pick and get started on Step 10.

The signs that this might be happening might be a loss of interest, a feeling of dragging on too long after you have already gotten all excited and interested about one or two of your beliefs on the list.

And if it turns out after you go ahead to Step 10 and the belief you started on wasn't yet ready to be resolved — well, that's what the steps are for, to help you sort out the best path. So you just go back to your list and work through from Step 8.

Chapter 12

Belief Change Exercise (BCE) Step 8

Refine the "Hot List" – Choose the Beliefs You Would Like to Change

**Belief Change
Exercise
Step 8**

**In a different color PEN
SCORE each
highlighted belief
0 - 10
on how <u>INTERESTED</u>
you are in changing
it for the better
or removing it
10 = TOTALLY INTERESTED
0 = NOT INTERESTED AT ALL**

Like Step 4, this is another step where you score your beliefs on a scale of 0–10, only this time regarding your motivation and interest in changing the belief, i.e., resolving or deactivating it so that this one no longer acts to limit that area of your life.

With a different colored pen, write the score next to each highlighted belief. For example, any belief that your attention is riveted on and you gravitate towards as being "the one" to start on receives a 10.

Scores of 7, 8, 9 may be given to those beliefs that strongly motivate you to eliminate their influence from your life.

A score of 5 is a "probably" or "maybe" and anything below it is left to handle later in the exercise if it remains significant or you are interested in dealing with it at that time.

0 of course goes to beliefs you have no interest at all in changing at this time. It would be rare for beliefs that score a 0 or even 1 or 2 to find their way through the procedure onto the final list.

By now you have asterisks, scores, slashes etc. on your different beliefs; and now you will focus on only those highlighted ones with a high score on wanting to change it. Remember that after you have applied BCE Step 10 to your chosen belief, you can still address any or all of the other beliefs later on. The whole point of the BCE is that you have the freedom to apply the Step 10 (BCE) to any belief you wish.

The purpose of first going through the earlier steps of the whole BCE (Steps 1– 9) is to make sure that you have the best chance possible of getting the one to start with that is going to give you the most benefit, the fastest.

At the end of this – Step 8 – you will have a fine-tuned list that you began back in Step 3. From the score written in a different colored pen, next to the highlighted beliefs, you will, in Step 9, select *"the one"* belief you will work on first with the sets of questions in Step 10!

Step 8 Action:

Consider each of these HIGHLIGHTED BELIEFS ONLY and score each on a scale of 0 – 10 as to how interested you are in changing it for the better. **Write the score beside them, on the left, in a different colored pen,** 10 being absolute total interest in changing it, 5 being "probably", "maybe", or "somewhat" and 0 being no interest at all.

Step 8 example: The scores on the highlighted beliefs were written on the left, and there are 4 beliefs scoring 8 and above. You could include the "7s" in your evaluation, but it's likely your final pick in Step 9 will be one of the "9s" or "10s", indicating an intense desire to change the belief for the better.

9   If I were affluent and prospering everyone would depend on me to support them – 8   *   ///// /

If I were affluent and prospering I would have to pay way too much taxes – 7   *   ////

8   *If I were* affluent and prospering people wouldn't like me for myself – 9   *   ///// //

If I were affluent and prospering I'd have nothing left to learn – 7   *   ///

If I were affluent and prospering I might lose my spirituality – 6

If I were affluent and prospering my kids would never learn how to become tough enough to handle adversity – 5

10   *If I were* affluent and prospering I'd never know whether people cared about me or the money – 8   *   ///// //

6   *If I were* affluent and prospering I might become really obnoxious to people who aren't – 7   *   ///// /

5   *If I had* consistent passive income I might get really lazy –   7 * ///// /

7   *If I had* consistent passive income I might lose my sense of purpose – 9   *   /////

If I had consistent passive income my kids might never learn how to make money and get wealthy themselves – 4

8   *If I had* consistent passive income I'd get complacent and lose my drive – 7   *   /////

Chapter 13

Belief Change Exercise (BCE) Step 9

Select the First Target

Belief Change Exercise Step 9

CHOOSE from HIGHEST SCORING BELIEFS the **ONE BELIEF** you are most interested in starting on first

CIRCLE IT AND DATE IT

Now is the time to pick from your highest scoring beliefs the one that you want to tackle first. Ideally you will then begin BCE Step 10 immediately after you identify the first target belief.

If you look over your "refined hot list" – Step 8 – and your first target belief to work on doesn't pop up fairly quickly, a way to help you to decide is to answer the question

"Which belief, when it is gone or its effects are diminished, would best help me achieve my goals or my ideal situation in this area?" Or you can go over it in more detail by addressing each belief on your list with the question, "What if this _(belief)_ no longer impacted my life?" Allow yourself to use visualization or sense which belief seems the most significant.

Once you have selected your first target belief to address, you circle it and write the date on it. The reason for the circle is clarity. The reason for the date is so that when you return to the list later, you can see what you picked and when you picked it.

Step 9 Action:

Choose the first belief for the Belief Change Exercise (BCE) application from your "Hot List" made on Step 7. **Consider all the beliefs with the highest score on your list, select the one you are most interested in working on right now, circle it and date it.**

Step 9 example: The choice here was scored with a "9" regarding interest in changing it, and was chosen over the two that scored a "10". There's nothing that says the one you choose to work on has to be one of the highest scoring. It may get chosen over a "10" because you may not be ready to tackle the highest scoring ones, and you might be more comfortable starting on a belief that's not so intense.

9 If I were affluent and prospering everyone would depend on me to support them — **8**
* ///// /

**If I were** affluent and prospering I would have to pay way too much taxes — 7 * ////

> **9 If I were affluent and prospering people wouldn't like me for myself – 9 * ///// // 4th April 2010**

**If I were** affluent and prospering I'd have nothing left to learn – **7** * ///

**If I were** affluent and prospering I might lose my spirituality – **6**

**If I had** were affluent and prospering my kids would never learn how to become tough enough to handle adversity – **5**

10 _**If I were**_ affluent and prospering I'd never know whether people cared about me or the money – **8** * ///// //

6 _**If I were**_ affluent and prospering I might become really obnoxious to people who aren't – **7** * ///// /

5 _**If I had**_ consistent passive income I might get really lazy – **7** * ///// /

7 _**If I had**_ consistent passive income I might lose my sense of purpose – **9** * /////

**If I had** consistent passive income my kids might never learn how to make money and get wealthy themselves – **4**

8 _**If I had**_ consistent passive income I'd get complacent and lose my drive – **7** * /////

Note: If it turns out that you do not have time to fully complete Step 10 immediately after selecting your target belief, revisit Step 9 before moving forward with Step 10. It is possible that you might lose interest in improving the one you just selected or have grown interested in working through a different one. Consequently, if there is a time lapse between Steps 9 and 10, and you find you're a little less motivated, you can quickly revisit your high scoring highlighted beliefs – using your Step 8 list – just in case one of the others is a new top target for change.

Chapter 14

Belief Change Exercise (BCE) Step 10

The Belief Re-Evaluation Step

Belief Change Exercise Step 10

Write out the answers to the 1st Set of questions 'til you feel it is complete; i.e., positive change of viewpoint on belief, new insight, "aha" moment or run out of answers. REPEAT PROCEDURE on SAME belief using next set of questions to **completion** Continue doing each set of questions 'til belief addressed is complete.

Yea! We are finally ready to begin the actual exercise of reevaluating your first target belief.

You spent the first 9 steps of the Belief Change Exercise finding the most appropriate belief to re-evaluate first. Now it's time to apply Step 10 to it. (This exercise can also be used to address beliefs found by other methods than the Belief Change Exercise laid out in the previous chapters.)

This step consists of 16 separate sets of questions, each of which is answered sequentially and in rotation until a completion is achieved on that particular set.

You can expect to be in a state of deep focus on your life, habits, behaviors, experiences and feelings as you answer the questions. This is good! It helps you to get the best out of the exercise.

As before, but especially now, it is important that you are awake, alert, and not distracted. There are certain guidelines that should be followed to get the best results. A previous chapter covered the preparation for applying this exercise, but a short summary in this section is timely.

If you are tired, exhausted or did not get your usual amount of sleep last night, it is not a good idea to tackle this until you are rested. When your body is trying to hibernate to update its systems it is not a good idea to force it to investigate your past – the two activities conflict! The overall effect is a lack of focus and an inability to dig deep into your issues without experiencing some degree of unconsciousness. It can also prevent you from realizing truths and experiencing relief because your body tends to hold onto negative energy when it is tired and not well slept.

If you are hungry, your attention will go onto that and your body will again try to hold onto energy, including the negative energy you are trying to remove by working this exercise. So do not do this exercise while hungry.

What you eat is important also. Make the foods you eat reasonably nutritious – candy, bread and French Fries are not activity-supporting nourishment and energy for this exercise.

Drugs and alcohol in general cloud your awareness. Also, they blanket access to real issues and negative energies. Do not go through this exercise on a day you drink alcohol; it is best to wait till the next day after drinking before doing this.

As far as drugs are concerned, even over-the-counter quick fixes such as headache medicines take several days to work their way out of your system and may limit your ability to complete the exercise effectively. Any drug, including prescription medicines, can impair the outcome! While it may seem a great idea to do this exercise while under the influence of the latest designer drug we strongly discourage it based on many years of experience. Some drugs can take weeks to work their way out of the system and heavy usage or even a steady intake of mild medication can affect your alertness more than you realize. Just listen to the side effects warnings on the TV ads to get an idea of that!

If you are going through a huge life crisis, even if you are doing the exercise to help with that, make sure it will not distract you from focusing on working the exercise.

Also, make sure you have at least 30 minutes to an hour or more scheduled to work through all of the questions in the exercise. Of course you can spend 2 or 3 hours at a time if you wish, remaining vigilant that you do not get tired or hungry. Food and restroom breaks are encouraged when needed!!!

One final consideration is the environment in which you will work. The ideal situation is when you know you will not be disturbed.

Interruptions, such as children, phones or background noise, are not conducive to intense and effective focus. You may want to hang a "Do not disturb under any circumstances except real emergency" sign on your door to insure privacy. If anyone asks what you are doing, and it affects them or they are entitled to know, tell them you found an exercise in a book that you want to try out and you must concentrate without interruptions so you would really appreciate it if they don't disturb you until you are finished with it.

All right! Now you are ready *and* prepared to give the exercise your best attention. You may wish to handwrite your answers. There are worksheets in the appendix at the back of the book that can be photocopied and used to work the exercise. The **www.beliefchangebook.com** website provides an online alternative for copies of the Belief Change Exercise worksheets. You can also use blank or notebook paper; however, we advise that you write the belief on the sheet along with the date and which set of questions you are answering.

About the Questions

The introspection part of the exercise involves you examining the record of your life and recalling the circumstances in which you were using or affected by the belief. It may take some time to get an answer, that's not the same as struggling when there is no answer to be got.

Don't worry about grammar or spelling mistakes, just write a summary, it does not have to be complete sentences as long as it makes sense to you.

If you only get one answer that is fine, if you get a whole avalanche that is fine too, write them all down. Generally speaking don't struggle to dig up answers if they don't flow easily after some focus and concentration.

***Set 1 Questions*:**

A/   What are the apparent benefits of this belief?

B/   What are the disadvantages of this belief?

This first set of two questions causes you to consider opposite aspects of your target belief. On Question A "What are the apparent benefits of the belief?" write down whatever answers come to mind about how this belief seems to have aided or protected you.

It may seem to you that there is not an apparent benefit; that is probably not true. There is always a perceived benefit somewhere deep down. With a deeply fixed belief that has been detrimental to your success, up until now, you *believed* the benefits were real and in your best interest. And maybe the belief did have real benefits for a short while, then once it became fixed the apparent benefits turned into prison bars.

So as you progress through Step 10, you will discover for yourself whether they were **really** benefits or in fact had a negative impact on your life. You are in the process of discovering the truth.

For example if the belief you are working on is *"If I were affluent everyone would depend on me to support them",* some benefits might be:
- "It keeps me from having to be responsible for my relatives"
- "It makes sure all my children are independent and self-reliant"
- "I'm much more free to do exactly what I want"
- "I don't have to face-up to people and stick to my guns and insist that they be financially viable in their own right"

On Question B in Sct 1 "What are the disadvantages of this belief?" you are looking for how the belief has held you back, kept you from expanding, and/or hindered you from achieving your ideal situation.

So, still using the belief *"If I were affluent everyone would depend on me to support them",* as an example, some disadvantages might be:

- "It stops me from really trying or trying hard"
- "It makes me give up really easily"
- "It makes me feel depressed about the future"
- "Keeps me from getting ahead financially"
- "I feel compelled to conceal my net worth from people in case they want something."
- "I don't trust people"
- "I don't have the courage to tell people that might want to borrow money that they should get themselves educated and make it themselves"
- "it supports me being a chicken"

After answering question B go back to question A and add any new answers that come to mind. Then back to B and add anything new for that question.

Answering these sets of questions, back and forth, is like peeling an onion. Once you uncover the first layer, it exposes the next layer with a new set of answers and new and deeper insights. That is the reason for going back and forth between the two questions until you reach what we call a *completion point.*

Completion Points

How do you know when you have reached the completion point on a set of questions? There is a list of the signs of having reached a completion point following each set of exercise questions.

The reason for having this list after each set of questions is so that you do not have to hunt around or turn to a different page looking for what they are as you answer the questions.

We will now expand on those indications so that you have as much information as possible to judge when you are done with a particular set of questions.

> One of the factors in reaching a completion point is the point when you experience *a positive change in your viewpoint* about the belief.

For example, you might suddenly feel certainty that you can change or have already changed the belief; or it may be that you feel more positive about your ideal situation and achieving it.

Or it may be that once surfaced, the belief now looks silly and ridiculous instead of serious and important.

Any of these experiences while answering a set of questions can mean that you have reached a completion point on that set of questions. (Please note that does not necessarily mean you have handled the belief for good. Usually it takes answering quite a number of sets of questions to completely disempower a heavy duty entrenched belief.)

> **Another signal of a completion point reached can be a noticeable *feeling of relief* from the negative energy attached to the belief.**

It is hard to describe what that feels like and there are a number of different versions of it.

It might manifest as a change between feeling stuck and fixated on the belief to a feeling of freedom and freed up attention.

It may show up as a lessening of tension in your body.

Or a feeling of optimism replacing pessimism, or lightness could replace heaviness.

A feeling of heaviness or seriousness as you answer the questions could suddenly disappear.

> **The next completion point sign is *gaining a new clarity on the belief.***

This may show up on its own or accompanied by some of the other signals.

What this means is that your perspective and understanding of the belief becomes more clear, sharp and focused as you inspect what it has been doing to your life in the Step 1 area you are addressing.

This completion sign most frequently shows up as a new awareness of how the belief has been reaching into your life like the tentacles of an octopus constraining and restricting you.

There will likely be many of these moments of new clarity as you continue to address the belief with many sets of questions.

You are clearing the fog from something that has previously been obscured from conscious awareness.

An example of a new clarity on a belief might be "I see that I have allowed this to stop me from better paying jobs because I was afraid I would be stuck with too much responsibility".

A completion point can be, simply put, a recognition of different ways the belief may have kept you trapped and small.

> **The "Aha!" moment is a very significant completion point or part of a completion point.**

This phenomenon is known in other arenas by different names such as an "epiphany" or realization; the essence of it is a sudden illumination in your awareness of something that's been previously hidden from you.

The definition of "realization" from the Merriam-Webster Dictionary[17] is:
  (1) a usually sudden manifestation or perception of the essential nature or meaning of something

(2) an intuitive grasp of reality through something (as an event) usually simple and striking

(3) **a:** an illuminating discovery, realization, or disclosure b : a revealing scene or moment.

Some examples of actual "Aha!" completion points for someone working the belief "if I could share my feelings easily and constructively, I might alienate or hurt people I love and care about," are:

- "I can practice sharing in a safe environment how to confront emotion effectively!"

    and

- "Nike: *just do it...* everything is uncomfortable until you've done it enough to get comfortable"

    and

- "It keeps people in my life that may not be healthy or aligned with my destiny and that keeps out people that are healthy and aligned with my destiny"

    and

- "Creates a comfort zone illusion for me"

    and

- "When I shatter this belief I will be tested and be required to put down the right answer. I don't believe I know the answer yet I have to be *out there, open, honest* and write down or speak the correct answer."

An important note is that "Aha!" moments, though they usually come as the result of answering the sets of questions, can also come later when you are doing something unrelated to the BCE.

> Sometimes it may be that before you reach any of the above completion points *you simply run out of answers.*

When you have considered both questions and have no more answers, do not struggle to dig up more. It is okay to move on to the next set of questions and "peel another layer off the onion".

Sooner or later, if you are on an interesting hot belief, changes will begin to occur and signs of completion should show up.

Addressing long held, strong and fixed beliefs can be quite challenging. After all they have often been running and maybe even wrecking your life up until now.

The key to successful redesign is facing up to it a bit at a time. You will work through this whole exercise piece by piece, so you can deal with it without getting overwhelmed.

The old joke about "how do you eat an elephant – one bite at a time," is a pretty good analogy for what you are doing here. In fact it is common knowledge that ants have killed elephants by doing just that!

Similarly this exercise helps you diminish your limiting beliefs "one bite at a time".

Note, if it does show up that there are more answers or more to be gained from a certain set of questions, there is no reason you cannot come back and work through them again if you are interested in doing so and get more benefit from it.

General notes on doing the BCE sets of questions – applies to all sets.

HANDLING RESISTANCE or DIFFICULTY

FACE IT & PUSH THROUGH if you were interested in **handling it in the first place** any **difficulty that shows up** is just part of the procedure of **viewing its effect on your life – PERSISTENCE** overcomes RESISTANCE

Resistance and even a reluctance to continue is not an unusual experience at this stage. In fact it is a natural protective response. Acknowledge your feelings, however persist through to the end.

Something to be aware of is that if you begin Step 10 full of interest, initially progress well and begin experiencing a changed perspective, and then things become uncomfortable or difficult, that does not necessarily mean you picked the wrong belief to work on. Because this belief has been negatively impacting your life for a long time, clearing it out can bring up uncomfortable aspects for you to view.

When addressing your fixed and limiting beliefs
PERSISTENCE OVERCOMES RESISTANCE
It is a good principle to follow!

The phenomenon of "very interested and shift is occurring" in Step 10 followed by a period of struggle while answering the questions is a good sign! You are coming to grips with the uninspected aspects of the belief. You are attaining mastery! The solution, therefore, is simple: persist and answer the questions even when uncomfortable.

> **Note:**
> If you notice changes occur in your thoughts and feelings regarding the belief then progress is being made. Even if you do not feel happy about what you see or learn about yourself. Continuing to explore and evaluate the belief should get you through to a changed perspective and more control over the belief..

Experiencing negative feelings and emotional energy that come up while addressing the belief – the one you are INTERESTED in changing – is not necessarily an indication that it is the wrong belief to start with. That would only be the case if after working on Step 10 for thirty minutes to an hour and nothing seems changed – no altered perspective at all, no insight into its effects on your life, just answering the questions and your interest in changing it has gone to zero. Unlikely though this is after going through the exercise which is designed to get you to the hot ones when properly done, if after persistence and diligence there is no change, simply return to Step 9, choose a different belief and begin Step 10 again.

> **Note:**
> Interest in bettering your life and changing your negative limiting and fixed beliefs is the energy that propels you through the procedures. The guidelines provided are the accumulated knowledge of what helps the exercise work and what has not worked in the past. The knowledge is founded on experience.

Set 2 questions of the BCE introduces a format of 4 questions, which will be used, with a variation of wording on each new set, throughout most of the remainder of the exercise.

We will now go over each question in Set 2, and most of what we cover will also apply to the remaining sets of 4.

Set 2 Questions:

A/ **In my life, what has this belief _____ stopped me from doing?**

B/ **In my life, what has this belief _____ made it OK for me to do?**

C/ **In my life, what has this belief _____ made it risky for me to do?**

D/ **In my life, what has this belief _____ made it safe for me to do?**

There are obvious distinctions between the different sets of 4. The questions remain fundamentally the same but each one addresses a different aspect of the belief's effects.

The same basic principles apply to all sets of questions as far as recording your answers and completion points goes.

Question A, "In my life what has this belief _____ stopped me from doing?" addresses a very wide scope of possibilities. On this question answers can range from

- "Achieving success"
- "Speaking my mind" to
- "Getting married" to
- "Trusting people" etc

It is probably one of the broadest questions used to address the belief.

Because beliefs *can* stop, limit, restrain, restrict, contain, hinder, prevent, slow you down, and many various aspects of "stop", answers to this question will likely come easily. Do not restrict yourself to writing just one answer if more than one shows up…

Question B, "In my life what has this belief _____ made it OK for me to do?" is a little trickier.

Some of the strongest things that show up on this question are actual restricted activities, or second rate or "second best" activities that a person gets involved in because the belief stops them from going all out for what they really want.

Some possible answers could be:
- "Stay in my comfort zone"
- "Lead a boring life"
- "Marry for convenience rather than wait for a meaningful romantic relationship"
- "Drop out of school"
- "Settle for second best"

Question C, "In my life what has this belief _____ made it risky for me to do?" is quite a crucial question. This is the one that tends to uncover all the things that you were afraid to do because of this belief. This question in itself can sometimes bring out even more deep-seated beliefs than Steps 1– 9 have revealed so far.

Typical answers that might show up:
- "Invest in the stock market"
- "Start a business"
- "Ask the prettiest girl in school out on a date"

Question D, "In my life what has this belief ___ made it safe for me to do?" usually reveals actions that shelter you in a cocoon; things that prevent your expansion and keep you small. Some examples might be:

- "Run away"
- "Hide"
- "Fume"
- "Bury my pain alive"
- "Hold back"
- "Hold my feelings in"

"Be comfortable." At this stage we need to cover the other sets of questions and the distinctions between the different sets of 4.

The fundamental set of questions is the same but each one addresses a different aspect of the belief's effects.

Set 3 of the questions are the same questions as the previous set but *"becoming"* is the theme addressed.

Set 3 Questions:

A/ **In my life, what has this belief** _____ **stopped me from becoming?**
B/ **In my life, what has this belief** _____ **made it OK for me to become?**
C/ **In my life, what has this belief** _____ **made it risky for me to become?**
D/ **In my life, what has this belief** _____ **made it safe for me to become?**

Question A, therefore, "In my life what has this belief ____ stopped me from becoming?" is addressing the identities and roles you may have been prevented from taking on as a result of the belief.

For example, if your belief is "If you are responsible for something you cannot delegate it," this belief may have prevented you from becoming:

- A big business owner
- An entrepreneur
- A company manager
- A leader

And, it may have made it okay for you to become

- A factory worker
- A follower
- A clerk
- A workaholic
- An assistant…

… if these were roles and identities you didn't actually want but took them on anyway as a result of the belief.

You will also probably have answers that may not necessarily reflect a role but rather encompass things like stopping you from becoming:

- Successful
- Effective
- Influential

……or making it OK for you to become:

- short-tempered
- stuck in a rut
- run down and tired

Set 4 questions address how the belief prevents you from *acquiring* or *owning* things, or even just being around people who have abundance.

Set 4 Questions:

A/   **In my life, what has this belief _____ stopped me from acquiring?**

B/   **In my life, what has this belief _____ made it OK for me to acquire?**

C/   **In my life, what has this belief _____ made it risky for me to acquire?**

D/   **In my life, what has this belief _____ made it safe for me to acquire?**

This can be a huge impact area for some people. There are many collective cultural beliefs around the area of success, finance and abundance that severely affect prosperity and goal achievement.

For example:

- Money is the root of all evil.
- Money doesn't grow on trees.
- You must work for a company that provides a good pension for retirement.
- It is more blessed to give than to receive.

So in answering the Set 4 questions you may find that a belief such as "if I have plenty of money and people find out they are going to want to take it from me" has made it risky to acquire things that might look like symbols of affluence such as:

- Investment real estate
- Luxury cars
- Stocks
- Ostentatious jewelry and so on…

It might also have made it safe to acquire

- Beat up or unattractive cars
- Low cost real estate
- Cheap jewelry

and other evidence that proves you don't have enough money for people to think there is anything there to separate you from!

Set 5 covers the area of *accomplishing* things, in other words achieving goals, having successes, completing projects, etc.

Set 5 Questions:

A/ **In my life, what has this belief _____ ____ stopped me from accomplishing?**

B/ **In my life, what has this belief _____ made it OK for me to accomplish?**

C/ **In my life, what has this belief _____ made it risky for me to accomplish?**

D/ **In my life, what has this belief _____ made it safe for me to accomplish?**

For example if you are addressing the belief, "If I were in a committed romantic relationship I mightn't be able to go out with my friends anymore", some of your answers about what that belief might stop you from accomplishing could encompass:

- Close relationships with people that attract you
- Long term relationships that might grow into permanent commitments
- A wild whirlwind romantic interlude
- A successful marriage
- Fatherhood or motherhood

And some of the things that it might allow or make it safe to accomplish might be as simple as:

- Becoming an expert flirt

- Becoming really good at some sport you participate in with your friends
- One night stands or short-lived flings

Or as profound as:

- Coolly friendly relationships with people that really attract you
- A steadily single uncommitted lifestyle; a bachelor existence

Set 6 covers the concept of *beginning or starting things*. What the belief stops you from beginning and what it makes okay to begin. The kinds of things that show up on this step are all about embarking on new projects, as well as activities and things that you have begun that are not what you really want to begin because the belief is stopping you from expanding to your full potential.

Set 6 Questions:

A/ **In my life, what has this belief _____ stopped me from beginning?**
B/ **In my life, what has this belief _____ made it OK for me to begin?**
C/ **In my life, what has this belief _____ made it risky for me to begin?**
D/ **In my life, what has this belief _____ made it safe for me to begin?**

Set 7 addresses *persistence* and how the belief hinders your persistence or allows you to persist with irrelevant or unimportant things. Beliefs can have a very strong effect on one's drive towards goals, and of course one of the key factors in achieving goals is persistence – hanging in there 'til you reach your goals.

Set 7 Questions:

A/ **In my life, what has this belief _____ stopped me from persisting with?**
B/ **In my life, what has this belief _____ made it OK for me to persist with?**

C/   **In my life, what has this belief _____ made it risky for me to persist with?**

D/   **In my life, what has this belief _____ made it safe for me to persist with?**

Set 8 covers the aspect of *finishing* things. Beliefs can have a profound effect on your ability to finish what you start, and the answers generally cover a multitude of things that lie around incomplete or activities that were never properly finished. The answers usually cover finishing things of little value as well as not finishing things of great value – the overall effect of your belief is to keep you focused on less than you can do.

Set 8 Questions:

A/   **In my life, what has this belief _____ stopped me from finishing?**

B/   **In my life, what has this belief _____ made it OK for me to finish?**

C/   **In my life, what has this belief _____ made it risky for me to finish?**

D/   **In my life, what has this belief _____ made it safe for me to finish?**

Set 9 questions look at how the belief might have impacted your *awareness*. Here you reach for previously hidden truths, and bring them into the light, so to speak, to see and understand their relevance compared to your current awareness and knowledge base.

Set 9 Questions:

A/   **In my life, what has this belief _____ stopped me from being aware of?**

B/   **In my life, what has this belief _____ made it OK for me to be aware of?**

C/   **In my life, what has this belief _____ made it risky for me to be aware of?**

D/   **In my life, what has this belief _____ made it safe for me to be aware of?**

This set also may expose distractions that the belief has caused you to be aware of, thereby diverting you off course instead of achieving your ideal situation. The Set 9 questions, thoroughly answered, can have a far-reaching effect in changing the belief.

Set 10 can also have a profound effect as it addresses what the belief has stopped you from *enjoying*. Many beliefs have a very deep-seated effect on your enjoyment of life and freedom to have fun. This set also exposes things that you might have enjoyed that have maybe served as a second rate substitute for what you would truly prefer to enjoy if you had your ideal situation.

Set 10 Questions:

A/ In my life, what has this belief _____ stopped me from enjoying?
B/ In my life, what has this belief _____ made it OK for me to enjoy?
C/ In my life, what has this belief _____ made it risky for me to enjoy?
D/ In my life, what has this belief _____ made it safe for me to enjoy?

Set 11 concentrates on what the belief has stopped you from focusing on or made it okay for you to focus on. This focus is a key factor in getting where you want to go and if a belief is strong enough to get you off the track it can have a significant effect. This set will cover many aspects of your life.

Set 11 Questions:

A/ In my life, what has this belief _____ stopped me from focusing on?
B/ In my life, what has this belief _____ made it OK for me to focus on?
C/ In my life, what has this belief _____ made it risky for me to focus on?
D/ In my life, what has this belief _____ made it safe for me to focus on?

Set 12 of the questions might well be the most impactful of all the sets because it involves a fundamental operating principle of life, facing up to things rather than running away. In fact the fundamental reason one adopts a belief is the failure or inability to actually confront something and deal with it effectively.

Set 12 Questions;

A/   In my life, what has this belief _____ stopped me from facing up to?

B/   In my life, what has this belief _____ made it OK for me to face up to?

C/   In my life, what has this belief _____ _ made it risky for me to face up to?

D/   In my life, what has this belief _____ made it safe for me to face up to?

The subject of Set 13 is a big issue for the human experience in general – *honesty, and saying what you are really thinking.* You may remember a movie starring Jim Carrey called "Liar, Liar". It is the story of a lawyer who, because of a wish made by his son, became incapable of telling a lie. The concept resonated so strongly in society that Oprah Winfrey devoted a couple of shows to the subject. For the show people attempted to tell the truth for a designated length of time and document their results. By all accounts it was very difficult and challenging to many of the participants.

So the questions about "What has this belief made it okay for me to say?" and "What has this belief made it risky for me to say?" can bring out the things that one has been afraid or embarrassed to communicate as well as the alterations of what you truly feel or think that you actually *did* say instead of the exact truth!

Set 13 Questions:

A/   In my life, what has this belief _____ stopped me from saying?

B/   In my life, what has this belief _____ made it OK for me to say?

C/   In my life, what has this belief _____ made it risky for me to say?

D/   In my life, what has this belief _____ made it safe for me to say?

Set 14, *getting involved* in things and activities, again covers the whole aspect of participation and expansion. Your answers will probably center around things that you chose to do but really didn't want to, times you settled for getting involved in something "second best", and things that you wished you had gotten involved with but didn't because the belief simply got in the way.

Set 14 Questions:

A/   **In my life, what has this belief _____ stopped me from getting involved in?**

B/   **In my life, what has this belief _____ made it OK for me to get involved in?**

C/   **In my life, what has this belief _____ made it risky for me to get involved in?**

D/   **In my life, what has this belief _____ made it safe for me to get involved in?**

Set 15, covers *success*. Those times the belief has stopped you from being successful or made it safe for you to be successful doing something second rate or different from what you really wanted.

Set 15 Questions:

A/   **In my life, what has this belief _____ stopped me from being successful at?**

B/   **In my life, what has this belief _____ made it OK for me to be successful at?**

C/   **In my life, what has this belief _____ made it risky for me to be successful at?**

D/   **In my life, what has this belief _____ made it safe for me to be successful at?**

Answers here can encompass how the belief stops you being successful, feeling success, or enjoying success when you have achieved it; what activities it stops you succeeding at; times you failed to "hit the mark"; and times you chose things that are safe to be successful at rather than going for bigger goals.

Step 16, to do with "indulging yourself", may cause a lot of people to cringe! Much of our cultural heritage can cause us to frown upon "indulging ourselves". For a lot of people it has overtones of decadence, "sin", depravity and negative or "bad" activities.

Certainly in today's society opportunities to indulge oneself have never been more available to the many. The problem is, there also are huge numbers of people who beat themselves up for indulging themselves in perfectly legitimate pleasures even if they have been highly productive and have earned it.

Set 16 questions:

A/   **In my life, what has this belief _____ stopped me from indulging myself in?**

B/   **In my life, what has this belief _____ made it OK for me to indulge myself in?**

C/   **In my life, what has this belief _____ made it risky for me to indulge myself in?**

D/   **In my life, what has this belief _____ made it safe for me to indulge myself in?**

There is no sin in pleasure as long as it does not harm others; though we are sure people with very solid beliefs to the contrary would disagree! But on this set of questions, you may find that whatever belief you are working on, it may have prevented you from indulging in a variety of activities pleasurable to you – or it may have made it OK for you to indulge in activities that are counter-productive to actually getting things done, such as acting like a victim, blaming others, justifying failures, self-pity, etc.

The belief may have made it unsafe to indulge in celebrations of achievements, fun activities, and made it safe to just indulge yourself in messing around, wasting time and not getting on with the important things of your life.

By the time you have reevaluated your belief through all of these questions, and gotten to a completion point on each of them, you should have experienced significant changes.

In some cases, before you get to Step 16, you may have come to the point where the power of the belief has become drastically minimized or simply disappeared.

There is no magic number of how many sets it takes to do this. There are several criteria for deciding a belief is as complete as you can get it then going off to test out how much change there is in your life.

You could suddenly find that you have gained an ability in the area that you did not have before using the BCE on the belief. Or you might find you have a big relief from the fixedness of the belief and have no further interest in working on it because it feels done.

Another possibility is that you feel quite different about the belief and your viewpoint is substantially changed.

Or you could experience a big win about the belief. At that point it is time to take a break and either take on another belief or go find out how your life has changed! One psychologist who worked through an earlier version of this exercise remarked on how tough it was for her to do, but that her life and finances had changed very much for the better as a result.

In general, as you go through the exercise, it's a good idea to write down your gains, benefits and wins. Record your changed viewpoints.

Then take a break and go find out if your life has changed for the better!

Chapter 15

What's next?

Very simply, once the belief you worked on has been disempowered, you use the exercise to pick another one you are highly interested in changing; then, do the BCE Step 10 on it. Metaphorically, continue to *peel the onion!* If you find that many of your Step 8 choices are no longer a priority to change, possibly because handling the first one collapsed a lot of the power out of them too, return to the consequences list you made in Step 3, start a new worksheet and re-score them afresh.

Generally, going back to Step 7 is far enough, just redo your scores on how much you want to change each belief, and take it from there.

What happens when the whole area shifts much closer to my ideal situation and some other area seems more interesting to explore?

That's when you begin Step 1 again, working on your new area, and apply the exercise to it!

What if... We Increase Your Chances for Success?

How many exciting and promising programs sit on shelves unused?

Who do you know that has, with great enthusiasm and high hopes, purchased a book, set of DVDs, CDs or online systems determined to make their life better in some significant positive way only to set it aside, never complete it, nor reap the anticipated rewards?

Ever wondered what you could buy with all those dollars you invested in self-development and still, you are metaphorically *climbing the same mountain* or *spinning your wheels*?

Don't feel bad, statistics tell us that you are among the majority! It is way too easy to get discouraged and give up when you try to master new skills. Significant life changes made alone or surrounded by people who do not understand or who do not have the ability to encourage or contribute to your efforts, challenge your conviction and persistence; sadly, without support it is human nature to quit.

Based on extensive experience and research, my co-author and I did everything we could to make our procedure simple; yet, we remain aware of those sad statistics. *That* defeats our goal! It totally defeats our purpose for writing this book. Therefore, determined to enable our readers' success, we studied *success models* – people who succeed learning, mastering and excelling at doing what they love.

When you think about professional athletes, particularly the highly successful ones, have you noticed that they all have coaches and personal trainers? How many hours do you imagine they invested preparing, practicing and receiving feedback on their performance to reach their peak potential?

The coach or personal trainer understands their client's goals and knows specific techniques that distinguish success from poor performance. They observe them in action, reinforce what is done right and deliver feedback to correct what is done less than optimum. Initially there is a lot of improvement to be made; however, with time and repetition, the new or improved skills get better and better until the *doing* becomes *second nature*. No longer do they have to consciously concentrate on each little detail of technique and form, rather, *doing* becomes *automatic*, a *habit*. Ultimately, those who persevere become superstars.

On a more personal note, can you remember back when as a child you struggled to learn to spell simple words like your name, the word "cat" or to think through the right answer to the math problem 2+2=_? If you can't remember what that was like, ask a 3-year-old "what does 2+2 equal?" There was a time when the concept was foreign and unnatural to you as well, probably when you, too, were 3-years-old. The same process that moved you *and* I as children learning simple math, from foreign and unnatural to familiar and second nature applies to learning and mastering any new skill, even to applying the BCE. Mastery is possible!

Recently I began Bikram Yoga[13] – "give me 90 minutes, every day, for 60 days and I guarantee you will not suffer back pain again," promised Jakob my first class instructor. This was especially meaningful to me because a mere 4 hours before my first class, I sprained my back – again! An annoying, chronic problem that I had tried countless medical and alternative treatments and exercises to heal; I eagerly tried anything short of surgery and drugs…, only to have it recur in the most inopportune times, like my first day at *this* Yoga class. I had tried Yoga several times before but as an amateur was quickly left behind, confused and ineffective; in frustration, I eventually quit.

Jakob and Sean, Jacob's alternate Bikram Yoga instructor, serve like a combination cheerleader, motivational speaker and technique coach – kind of like a *team trainer*. However, their skills are most impressive and most importantly *effective*. Unlike previous classes in Yoga or other "coaching programs" where some succeed while others, like me, unsuccessfully mastered the skills or concepts to be developed, these young men master skill transference for the entire group from beginning to end. Although there are between 15 and 20 students in each class, with skills and flexibility ranging from expert to first-timers as well as every level in between, they identify each of us, level set us then successfully coach each of us from inability to ability in an impressively short time. They encourage us collectively, while comprehending our level of capability individually and manage to provide the perfect instruction at the exact right time. Many times, when I found myself frustrated and discouraged, ready to give up, their compassionate coaxing and technique coaching encouraged me to stretch my comfort zone and successfully reach a new level of ability. Our program works similarly.

The Belief Change Facilitation Program - Your Personal Success Coach

Now, like the superstars and *me*, you too have access to personal training, at reasonable and affordable prices! Our *Belief Change Facilitation* program offers encouragement, *trained* facilitation and support. You can choose to learn and master these skills with feedback and instruction from your very own personal coach.

The key to our program's success is *trained* facilitators. Not only do they have the knowledge, skills and abilities to educate and coach in a *hot* environment, like my Bikram Yoga instructors Jakob and Sean, they create a safe space for you to share your most vulnerable thoughts and embarrassing experiences without fear of judgment or concern for privacy. All trained facilitators are tested and must demonstrate that they can adhere to our program's code of conduct before they work with clients or stu-chers[14] – people who are both *stu*dents and tea*chers*. They know the business! For more information and to register, please visit the website: **www.BeliefChangeBook.com**

You Learn Best What You Teach…

Additional options include a virtual community of "stu-chers", very much like you, with similar goals and challenges, helping and encouraging each other.

How does that work? In his seminars, Stephen Covey[15] teaches that when you learn something new you should teach it three times within 24 hours. What this does is help your mind to fully assimilate, understand and integrate the concept behind the subject. This lays the foundation for *mastery*.

For participation in the Belief Change Facilitation Program you will be assigned to a trained and certified facilitator (coach), he or she will help you learn and understand the process. Then, if you choose to enter the next level you train and gain certification as well. Advancement is a two part process that promotes and enhances skill integration and transference:

1. You study and demonstrate facilitator skills

2. You train and facilitate your coach through the BCE three times

Once you become certified and demonstrate effective facilitation skills you are then qualified for step 3

3. You work as an apprentice facilitator for *supervised* facilitation of at least three new entries into the Belief Change Facilitation Program.

After you become a fully trained and certified facilitator, not only will you experience the benefit of having resolved some personal self-sabotaging and defeating beliefs along the way, but you also integrate your newly acquired skills – they become a *habit*. For many of us, it really feels good to help others, especially our friends and family, like we feel we were helped. Ultimately, then, helping others move closer to their personal dreams, fulfillment and life mastery continues to enhance, polish and fine tune your own personal skills and life mastery.

In summary, the benefits and advantages to participation in the Belief Change Facilitation Program include:

- Completely safe environment and relationships to release old stuff, learn new *stuff*, grow and reach your personal goals.
- Dialog improves clarity and understanding. You will know exactly what to do to blast through beliefs that limit, and even those that stop dead, your hopes, dreams and heart's desires.
- Feedback, encouragement and accountability improve odds of successfully living your ideal scenario.
- Becoming a stu-cher integrates what you learn/teach so that it becomes second nature and *mastered!*
- It can feel really good to help others learn what you learned and benefit as you benefited.

For more information and to register, please visit the website: **www.BeliefChangeBook. com**

One final consideration, it has been said that if you want to increase your income, raise your standard of living or otherwise make a significant change in your life's circumstances – literally replace your friends. Choose people who already do what you want to do. Andrew Carnegie, as told to Napoleon Hill and recorded in the book *Think and Grow Rich*[16], attributed much of his success to his "Mastermind Group". A highly successful and diverse group of businessmen in his community, they met weekly to share their ideas and activities. It was their way of refining, polishing or otherwise *fine tune* their various business endeavors.

What would you be, do or have if you became a superstar at handling every circumstance, condition or interaction in your life experience? How would your life be different if you knew what you wanted, asked for it and actually received it? Which relationships would be most improved for you if old emotional baggage was dissolved and hurt feelings healed?

Conclusion

When your belief system is aligned with your goals and aspirations you become a powerful magnet that *attracts* what you want *to you*. This does not mean you no longer play a role in the manifestation or that everything just happens without any action on your part. What it does mean is that you respond and act on what shows up in your life, and there should be much less struggle in the area(s) you addressed.

For example, if your heart's desire is to have a successful and expanding business, it is you who

1. Starts up or buys a business.
2. Organize1s and manages it .
3. Trains people to operate it.
4. Pays attention to its production and operation.
5. Corrects, adjust and modifies it as needed.

Removal of fixed beliefs that work against business success can make it easier, challenging but fun. Yet, your action is still an essential ingredient.

Just in case you wonder – yes, Step 10 can be used to desensitize or remove beliefs surfaced other than through Steps 1 to 9 above. If they are "hot" and interesting, begin at Step 4 and move through Step 10. If there is only one, begin with Step 10.

When you are ready for an experienced, trained facilitator to maintain your confidence and help you through the exercise, as mentioned before; it is available. For information on those services available, please visit the website: **www.BeliefChangeBook.com**

Additional Resource Websites:
> **www.thesecretsolution.net**
> **www.mastermindcleanse.com**

Appendix A

Belief Change Exercise
The Action Steps

Following are the 10 steps of the exercise plus instructions in sequence to make it easier to work through. There is no theory nor are there examples. If a question arises, please refer to information found in the correlating previous chapters.

Before beginning this exercise make sure you are well fed and rested, and won't be disturbed while you are doing it. The exercise works best if you are not on medication or haven't just come from "Happy Hour", i.e. drugs and alcohol can reduce your ability to focus and get the best results!

BCE Step 1

Action: CHOOSE TARGET AREA FOR POTENTIAL IMPROVEMENT.

Choose an area of your life (or two at the most) where you have:
- constant problems
- obvious repeating pattern
- an area you would most like to change or improve
- an area that you have worked on and it did not resolve

If you are using the worksheet from the appendix or the website, fill in the appropriate blank; otherwise, write across the top of a clean sheet of paper or begin a new word processing document in your computer with your target area.

Example areas to choose from:

- Abilities
- Money and Wealth
- Physical Well-being and Health
- Relationships, including Family, Children, & Business relationships
- Lifestyle
- Business
- Work or Career
- Team or Group Co-operation
- Success and Goal Achievement
- Personal Growth
- Self Esteem and Self Confidence
- Spirituality
- Education and Learning
- Satisfaction and Fulfillment
- Adaptability and Flexibility
- Excitement
- Motivation and Passion
- Age and Aging
- Appearance and image
- Order and managing disorder
- Commitment and keeping agreements
- Responsibility and accountability
- Delegation
- Leadership
- Competence and effectiveness
- Friends

- Community
- Nutrition
- Weight or size
- Correcting or handling mistakes
- Wisdom and maturity
- Organization and systems
- Possessions
- Intelligence and mental abilities
- Love
- Sex life and sexual well-being
- Romance
- Power
- Persistence & follow-through
- Ability to market and sell
- Acceptance and belonging
- Trust of self & others
- Time management & time agreements
- Achieving emotional balance & healthy emotional expression
- Ability to experience and express feelings
- Production & Productivity
- Creativity
- Happiness
- Ability to change with the times
- Ability to learn from your mistakes
- Ability to effectively change and improve your life
- Contribution to society
- Stress and reactions to stress
- Ability to face up to unpleasant realities

BCE Step 2

Action: DESCRIBE YOUR IDEAL SITUATION IN YOUR CHOSEN AREA

List out how you want your life to be in that area.

My ideal situation regarding my chosen area _____ is:

- *I will be…*
- *I will do…*
- *I will have…*

BCE Step 3

Action: LIST POSITIVE AND NEGATIVE CONSEQUENCES OF ACHIEVING YOUR IDEAL SITUATION

List possible consequences, positive (+) and negative or limiting (−), you feel there might be if you achieved each of the ideal situations or goals you listed in Step 2.

The general format to follow is:

If I were/did/had _____ (my ideal situation from Step 2) *the consequences would be* _____

Mark each statement + or − then <u>underline the negative ones</u>. The <u>negative statements</u> will be the ones used in the following steps of this exercise.

BCE Step 4

Action: RATE HOW FIXED EACH BELIEF IS

Score each of the listed <u>negative</u> (underlined) consequences from 0 to 10 as to how fixed it is or how confident you are that it is true. You may ask yourself:

"How true, certain or real is this possible consequence?" and grade it accordingly. Or, "How easily could you change your mind about it and cease to believe it is true, or cease to act on it?"

A "0" score means it is not fixed at all or you don't really believe it, "10" indicates you believe it is a fundamental truth of the universe! You might rate it 5 if you believe it isn't true but you don't think you can change it by just deciding it isn't true. Write the score beside each.

BCE Step 5

Action: IDENTIFY THE MOST FIXED OF THE NEGATIVE BELIEFS

Considering each of your underlined and scored beliefs, mark with an asterisk * the beliefs that scored the highest.

For your first time through the BCE, try to select a reasonable number of possible beliefs which you will then evaluate further in Step 6.

Typically you might include those with scores at least 6 and above; however, if you have a lot of 9s and 10s then those would probably be all you would mark. You do want a reasonable selection but do not want too many or Step 6 will take too long.

BCE Step 6

Action: DETERMINE IMPACT OF YOUR FIXED BELIEFS ON YOUR LIFE

Ask and answer the following 7 questions about each asterisked belief on your "Consequences List". For each "yes" answer make a slash mark (/) beside the belief. Leave a "no" answer unmarked. You may end up with as many as 7 slashes (///// //) beside each of the beliefs marked with an asterisk* or as few as 0.

1. **Does this belief** _____ **hold you back from doing what you want or making progress towards your goals?**

2. **Does this belief** _____ **prevent you from facing up to an area of your life and dealing with it?**

3. **Does this belief** _____ **seem to solve some problem area in your life?**

4. **Does this belief** _____ **seem to you to be so true that you can't imagine how your life would be if you didn't believe it or if you found out it wasn't true?**

5. **Does this belief** _____ **seem to stop you from thinking logically and rationally about your target area of difficulty as well as working out how to handle it?**

6. **Has this belief** _____ **caused you to feel you are a little better than other people?**

7. **Has this belief** _____ **had an effect of making other people feel put down or less than you?**

BCE Step 7

Action: **CREATE THE "HOT LIST" – THE BELIEFS WITH THE MOST IMPACT ON YOUR LIFE**

Select the highest scoring beliefs from Step 6 and mark each one with a highlighter.

Any beliefs that tally 7 out of 7 slash marks are on your "hot list." So are the ones with 6. But if your highest scoring beliefs are only "4s" and "5s", for example, that's fine – mark those beliefs with a highlighter.

Your final selection must be extensive enough for you to evaluate the one you are going to work on first, and not so big that it is overwhelming. *If* you only have a couple with 7 slashes on your list, for this step include your "6's" and maybe "5's" as well. Beliefs with 4 or 5 slash marks only become significant if you have none with 6 or 7.

At the end of this step you have a fine-tuned list from the one you began back in Step 3. It typically might have anywhere from 5 to 20 highlighted negative beliefs.

BCE Step 8

Action: **REFINE THE "HOT LIST" – CHOOSE THE BELIEFS YOU'D LIKE TO CHANGE**

Considering each of these highest-scoring beliefs, on a scale of 0 – 10, rate how interested you are in changing this belief for the better. Using colored pens, write the score beside each in a different color. 10 representing absolute total interest - 5 being "probably" or "maybe" - 0 meaning no interest at all.

BCE Step 9

Action: SELECT YOUR FIRST TARGET

Choose the first belief for Belief Change Exercise application from your Step 8 List.

Read through your hot list, if your first target belief to work on doesn't pop up fairly quickly, a way to help you to decide is to answer the question, "Which belief, when it is gone or its effects are diminished, would best help me achieve my goals or my ideal situation in this area?" Or you can go over it in more detail by addressing each belief on your list with the question, "What if this _(belief)_ no longer impacted my life or my current situation in this area?" Trust your intuition or "gut feeling" to select which belief to work first.

Select the belief you are most interested in working on right now, circle it and date it.

BCE Step 10

Action: RE-EVALUATE THE TARGETED BELIEF.

Prepare: When you have at least 30 minutes to concentrate on this part of the exercise, take a clean sheet of paper, or open a new file in your computer; then, settle yourself in a quiet place where you will be undisturbed and begin to discover and write the answers to these questions. (Note – do not begin step 10 if you notice that you are now tired or hungry – fix that first or start again when you are fresh!)

On a clean sheet of paper write out, in full, the selected first target belief ("the belief that _____"). Clip this paper on the top of the question sheet where you can see it as you write the answers to the following sets of questions.

For each question write as many or as few answers that come to mind easily then go to the next question and do the same. Cycle through A, B, A, B, A etc or A, B, C, D, A, B, C, D, A, etc, and add new answers till you reach completion. You will know you are complete on the set of questions when you experience a positive change in your viewpoint concerning the belief, or feel a sense of relief or lightness, or experience a new clarity on the belief, have an "Aha!" moment (realize something you weren't previously aware of, negative or positive – write those down) or you run out of answers.

Note: you are not meant to struggle to find answers. Look for them, investigate, consider the question carefully, but if no answers are coming to mind, move on to the next question. Sometimes the first cycle through you may have no answers for a question yet on a subsequent cycle new answers show up.

Use extra sheets of paper as needed and add them to your first page.

Set 1 Questions

A/ What are the apparent benefits of this belief?

Write as many or as few answers as show up easily.

B/ What are the disadvantages of this belief?

Write as many or as few answers as show up easily.

Now go back and forth, A, B, A, B, etc, adding to your answers on each question until you

- *experience a positive change in your viewpoint concerning the belief,*
- *OR you feel a feeling of relief,*

- *OR you have a new clarity on the belief*
- *OR you have an "Aha!" moment (write it down)*
- *OR you run out of answers.*

Set 2 Questions

A/   **In my life, what has this belief** _____ **stopped me from doing?**

Write as many or as few answers as show up easily.

B/   **In my life, what has this belief** _____ **made it OK for me to do?**

Write as many or as few answers as show up easily.

C/   **In my life, what has this belief** _____ **made it risky for me to do?**

Write as many or as few answers as show up easily.

D/   **In my life, what has this belief** _____ **made it safe for me to do?**

Write as many or as few answers as show up easily.

Now continue going through the questions in sequence A, B, C, D, A, B, C, D, A, etc., adding to your previous answers for each of them until you

- *experience a positive change in your viewpoint concerning the belief;*
- *OR you feel a feeling of relief;*
- *OR you have a new clarity on the belief;*
- *OR you have an "Aha!" moment;*
- *OR you run out of answers.*

Set 3 Questions

A/   **In my life, what has this belief** _____ **stopped me from becoming?**

Write as many or as few answers as show up easily.

B/   **In my life, what has this belief _____ made it OK for me to become?**

Write as many or as few answers as show up easily.

C/   **In my life, what has this belief _____ made it risky for me to become?**

Write as many or as few answers as show up easily.

D/   **In my life, what has this belief _____ made it safe for me to become?**

Write as many or as few answers as show up easily.

Now continue going through the questions in sequence A, B, C, D, A, B, C, D, A, etc., adding to your previous answers for each of them until you

- *experience a positive change in your viewpoint concerning the belief;*
- *OR you feel a feeling of relief;*
- *OR you have a new clarity on the belief;*
- *OR you have an "Aha!" moment;*
- *OR you run out of answers.*

Set 4 Questions

A/   **In my life, what has this belief _____ stopped me from acquiring?**

Write as many or as few answers as show up easily.

B/   **In my life, what has this belief _____ made it OK for me to acquire?**

Write as many or as few answers as show up easily.

C/   **In my life, what has this belief _____ made it risky for me to acquire?**

Write as many or as few answers as show up easily.

D/   **In my life, what has this belief _____ made it safe for me to acquire?**

Write as many or as few answers as show up easily.

Now continue going through the questions in sequence A, B, C, D, A, B, C, D, A, etc., adding to your previous answers for each of them until you

- *experience a positive change in your viewpoint concerning the belief;*
- *OR you feel a feeling of relief;*
- *OR you have a new clarity on the belief;*
- *OR you have an "Aha!" moment;*
- *OR you run out of answers.*

Set 5 Questions

A/ **In my life, what has this belief _____ stopped me from accomplishing?**

Write as many or as few answers as show up easily.

B/ **In my life, what has this belief _____ made it OK for me to accomplish?**

Write as many or as few answers as show up easily.

C/ **In my life, what has this belief _____ made it risky for me to accomplish?**

Write as many or as few answers as show up easily.

D/ **In my life, what has this belief _____ made it safe for me to accomplish?**

Write as many or as few answers as show up easily.

Now continue going through the questions in sequence A, B, C, D, A, B, C, D, A, etc., adding to your previous answers for each of them until you

- *experience a positive change in your viewpoint concerning the belief;*
- *OR you feel a feeling of relief;*
- *OR you have a new clarity on the belief;*
- *OR you have an "Aha!" moment;*
- *OR you run out of answers.*

Set 6 Questions

A/   In my life, what has this belief _____ stopped me from beginning?

Write as many or as few answers as show up easily.

B/   In my life, what has this belief _____ made it OK for me to begin?

Write as many or as few answers as show up easily.

C/   In my life, what has this belief _____ made it risky for me to begin?

Write as many or as few answers as show up easily.

D/   In my life, what has this belief _____ made it safe for me to begin?

Write as many or as few answers as show up easily.

Now continue going through the questions in sequence A, B, C, D, A, B, C, D, A, etc., adding to your previous answers for each of them until you

- *experience a positive change in your viewpoint concerning the belief;*
- *OR you feel a feeling of relief;*

- *OR you have a new clarity on the belief;*
- *OR you have an "Aha!" moment;*
- *OR you run out of answers.*

Set 7 Questions

A/   **In my life, what has this belief _____ stopped me from persisting with?**

Write as many or as few answers as show up easily.

B/   **In my life, what has this belief _____ made it OK for me to persist with?**

Write as many or as few answers as show up easily.

C/   **In my life, what has this belief _____ made it risky for me to persist with?**

Write as many or as few answers as show up easily.

D/   **In my life, what has this belief _____ made it safe for me to persist with?**

Write as many or as few answers as show up easily.

Now continue going through the questions in sequence A, B, C, D, A, B, C, D, A, etc., adding to your previous answers for each of them until you

- *experience a positive change in your viewpoint concerning the belief;*
- *OR you feel a feeling of relief;*
- *OR you have a new clarity on the belief;*

- *OR you have an "Aha!" moment;*
- *OR you run out of answers.*

Set 8 Questions

A/ **In my life, what has this belief _____ stopped me from finishing?**

Write as many or as few answers as show up easily.

B/ **In my life, what has this belief _____ made it OK for me to finish?**

Write as many or as few answers as show up easily.

C/ **In my life, what has this belief _____ made it risky for me to finish?**

Write as many or as few answers as show up easily.

D/ **In my life, what has this belief _____ made it safe for me to finish?**
Write as many or as few answers as show up easily.

Now continue going through the questions in sequence A, B, C, D, A, B, C, D, A, etc., adding to your previous answers for each of them until you

- *experience a positive change in your viewpoint concerning the belief;*
- *OR you feel a feeling of relief;*
- *OR you have a new clarity on the belief;*
- *OR you have an "Aha!" moment;*
- *OR you run out of answers.*

Set 9 Questions

A/ **In my life, what has this belief _____ stopped me from being aware of?**

Write as many or as few answers as show up easily.

B/   **In my life, what has this belief _____ made it OK for me to be aware of?**

Write as many or as few answers as show up easily.

C/   **In my life, what has this belief _____ made it risky for me to be aware of?**

Write as many or as few answers as show up easily.

D/   **In my life, what has this belief _____ made it safe for me to be aware of?**

Write as many or as few answers as show up easily.

Now continue going through the questions in sequence A, B, C, D, A, B, C, D, A, etc., adding to your previous answers for each of them until you

- *experience a positive change in your viewpoint concerning the belief;*
- *OR you feel a feeling of relief;*
- *OR you have a new clarity on the belief;*
- *OR you have an "Aha!" moment;*
- *OR you run out of answers.*

Set 10 Questions

A/   **In my life, what has this belief _____ stopped me from enjoying?**

Write as many or as few answers as show up easily.

B/   **In my life, what has this belief _____ made it OK for me to enjoy?**

Write as many or as few answers as show up easily.

C/   **In my life, what has this belief _____ made it risky for me to enjoy?**

Write as many or as few answers as show up easily.

D/   In my life, what has this belief _____ made it safe for me to enjoy?

Write as many or as few answers as show up easily.

Now continue going through the questions in sequence A, B, C, D, A, B, C, D, A, etc., adding to your previous answers for each of them until you

- *experience a positive change In your viewpoint concerning the belief;*
- *OR you feel a feeling of relief;*
- *OR you have a new clarity on the belief;*
- *OR you have an "Aha!" moment;*
- *OR you run out of answers.*

Set 11 Questions

A/   In my life, what has this belief _____ stopped me from focusing on?

Write as many or as few answers as show up easily.

B/   In my life, what has this belief _____ made it OK for me to focus on?

Write as many or as few answers as show up easily.

C/   In my life, what has this belief_____ made it risky for me to focus on?

Write as many or as few answers as show up easily.

D/   In my life, what has this belief _____ made it safe for me to focus on?

Write as many or as few answers as show up easily.

Now continue going through the questions in sequence A, B, C, D, A, B, C, D, A, etc., adding to your previous answers for each of them until you

- *experience a positive change in your viewpoint concerning the belief;*
- *OR you feel a feeling of relief;*
- *OR you have a new clarity on the belief;*
- *OR you have an "Aha!" moment;*
- *OR you run out of answers.*

Set 12 Questions

A/ **In my life, what has this belief _____ stopped me from facing up to?**

Write as many or as few answers as show up easily.

B/ **In my life, what has this belief _____ made it OK for me to face up to?**

Write as many or as few answers as show up easily.

C/ **In my life, what has this belief _____ made it risky for me to face up to?**

Write as many or as few answers as show up easily.

D/ **In my life, what has this belief _____ made it safe for me to face up to?**

Write as many or as few answers as show up easily.

Now continue going through the questions in sequence A, B, C, D, A, B, C, D, A, etc., adding to your previous answers for each of them until you

- *experience a positive change in your viewpoint concerning the belief;*
- *OR you feel a feeling of relief;*
- *OR you have a new clarity on the belief;*
- *OR you have an "Aha!" moment;*

- *OR you run out of answers.*

Set 13 Questions

A/ **In my life, what has this belief _____ stopped me from saying?**

Write as many or as few answers as show up easily.

B/ **In my life, what has this belief _____ made it OK for me to say?**

Write as many or as few answers as show up easily.

C/ **In my life, what has this belief _____ made it risky for me to say?**

Write as many or as few answers as show up easily.

D/ **In my life, what has this belief _____ made it safe for me to say?**

Write as many or as few answers as show up easily.

Now continue going through the questions in sequence A, B, C, D, A, B, C, D, A, etc., adding to your previous answers for each of them until you

- *experience a positive change in your viewpoint concerning the belief;*
- *OR you feel a feeling of relief;*
- *OR you have a new clarity on the belief;*
- *OR you have an "Aha!" moment;*
- *OR you run out of answers.*

Set 14 Questions

A/ **In my life, what has this belief _____ stopped me from getting involved in?**

Write as many or as few answers as show up easily.

B/   In my life, what has this belief _____ made it OK for me to get involved in?

Write as many or as few answers as show up easily.

C/   In my life, what has this belief _____ made it risky for me to get involved in?

Write as many or as few answers as show up easily.

D/   In my life, what has this belief _____ made it safe for me to get involved in?

Write as many or as few answers as show up easily.

Now continue going through the questions in sequence A, B, C, D, A, B, C, D, A, etc., adding to your previous answers for each of them until you

- *experience a positive change in your viewpoint concerning the belief;*
- *OR you feel a feeling of relief;*
- *OR you have a new clarity on the belief;*
- *OR you have an "Aha!" moment;*
- *OR you run out of answers.*

Set 15 Questions

A/   In my life, what has this belief _____ stopped me from being successful at?

Write as many or as few answers as show up easily.

B/ In my life, what has this belief _____ made it OK for me to be successful at?

Write as many or as few answers as show up easily.

C/ In my life, what has this belief _____ made it risky for me to be successful at?

Write as many or as few answers as show up easily.

D/ In my life, what has this belief _____ made it safe for me to be successful at?

Write as many or as few answers as show up easily.

Now continue going through the questions in sequence A, B, C, D, A, B, C, D, A, etc., adding to your previous answers for each of them until you

- *experience a positive change in your viewpoint concerning the belief;*
- *OR you feel a feeling of relief;*
- *OR you have a new clarity on the belief;*
- *OR you have an "Aha!" moment;*
- *OR you run out of answers.*

Set 16 Questions

A/ In my life, what has this belief _____ stopped me from indulging in?

Write as many or as few answers as show up easily.

B/ In my life, what has this belief _____ made it OK for me to indulge in?

Write as many or as few answers as show up easily.

C/ **In my life, what has this belief** _____ **made it risky for me to indulge in?**

Write as many or as few answers as show up easily.

D/ **In my life, what has this belief** _____ **made it safe for me to indulge in?**

Write as many or as few answers as show up easily.

Now continue going through the questions in sequence A, B, C, D, A, B, C, D, A, etc., adding to your previous answers for each of them until you

- *experience a positive change in your viewpoint concerning the belief;*
- *OR you feel a feeling of relief;*
- *OR you have a new clarity on the belief;*
- *OR you have an "Aha!" moment;*
- *OR you run out of answers.*

Appendix B

References & Acknowledgements:

[1] p 5, **Rhonda Byrne**, *The Secret*, "Law of Attraction" http://www.thesecret.tv/index.html

[2] p. 6, **Eckhart Tolle**, *The Power of Now,* 1997; and *A New Earth*, 2005 http://www.eckharttolle.com/eckharttolle

[3] p 9 , **SuperLearning,** is a system of teaching that speeds and optimizes learning by involving both sides of the brain as well as the senses. SuperLearning therefore includes many elements such as music, flip charts with colored pictures and text, games, exercises, and many questions from the presenter to keep the participants involved in the learning process.

[4] p 12, **Anthony Robbins**, "World Authority on Leadership Psychology", http://www.tonyrobbins.com/ *Personal Power* 1986; *Awaken the Giant Within,* 1991

[5] p 13, **Ego**: We acknowledge there are many applications for the term "ego". For our purposes we define the *function* of "ego" as follows: that part of human life, likely existing within the "mind" and serving as its "gatekeeper". As such, an "event" causes it to sort through files in its database to apply *meaning* to the "event" and initiate appropriate "action"[5]. Ego's objective is to protect its human from danger and pain – *survival.* For more on ego and its role in human life, visit www.thesecretsolution.net.

[6] p 14, **Additional source of scientific information**: www.answerbag.com/q_view/23027 & www.scienceagogo.com/news/19980428032910data_trunc_sys.shtml

[7] p 14, **Louise Hay**, http://www.louisehay.com/ *Heal Your Body,* 1976, Hay House, Inc.

[8] p 16, How Ego works: In approximately 300 milliseconds, the ego sorts through your database of experiences, locates all similar ones; then, the belief is either reinforced or invalidated creating either a positive or negative emotional-electrical charge which takes an additional 200 to 350 milliseconds.

When reinforced it stacks the judgments and decisions made upon the previous judgments and decisions and stores any perceived relevant details forming the filter through which you *understand* the event. The total process takes between 550 and 750 milliseconds[3]! How long is a millisecond? Answer, 1 thousandth (1/1000) of a second or really, really, really fast! It is no wonder you can sort and categorize the data associated to an event and *seem* to act without thinking – foundation of a habit.

[9] p 20, **magnet metaphor**; for purposes of this book we refer to the metaphysical concept of "like attracts like" and "opposites repel"

[10] p 20, **New Thought,** Law of Attraction, http://en.wikipedia.org/wiki/Law_of_Attraction

[11] p 29, **Barbara De Angelis, Ph.D.,** http://www.barbaradeangelis.com/

[12] p 39, **Alice's Adventures in Wonderland,** Lewis Caroll, 1865, Chapter Six

[13] p 108, **Bikram Yoga,** http://en.wikipedia.org/wiki/Bikram_Yoga and http://www.bikramyoga.com/

[14] p 110, **"stu-cher"** - term I heard somewhere in one of the many seminars I've attended, meaning that we are, or can be, both students and teachers in every life experience.

[15] p 110, **Dr. Stephen R. Covey**, *7 Habits of Highly Effective People*, 1989 https://www. stephencovey.com/

[16] p 112, ***Think and Grow Rich***, Napoleon Hill, 1937, Step 9

[17] p 80 "realization." Merriam-Webster Online Dictionary. 2007.Merriam-Webster Online. 29 August 2007<http://www.merriam-webster.com/dictionary/realization>

Worksheet 1

Step 1:

Target Improvement Area Selected: _____

Step 2:

List what you will *be*, *do* and *have* when you achieve the ideal in the area you selected.

-
-
-
-
-
-
-
-
-
-
-
-
-

Worksheet 2

Step 3

List, in the spaces provided below, next to ( ), all possible consequences, positive (+) and negative or limiting (–), you imagine there might be when you achieve your ideal situations or goals listed in Step 2. (Use back of page for additional consequences.)

The general format to follow is:

If I were/did/had _____ (my ideal situation from Step 2) the consequences would be _____
_____

Mark each statement either + or – then <u>underline the negative ones</u>. The <u>negative statements</u> will be the ones used in the steps to follow.

( )

( )

( )

( )

( )

( )

( )

( )

( )

( )

( )

( )

( )

( )

( )

( )

( )

( )

Coaching Program and Workshop information and registration:
www.BeliefChangeBook.com

Additional Resources:
www.TheSecretSolution.net
www.MasterMindCleanse.com

Next up for KISS (Keep It Simple Series):

Karma Change – *The Book How to Transmute Karma and Live the Life of Your Dreams*